the seven confLicts

Resolving the Most Common

Disagreements in Marriage

the seven confLicts

Tim *and* Joy Downs

MOODY PUBLISHERS
CHICAGO

Library of Congress Cataloging-in-Publication Data

Downs, Tim.
    The seven conflicts : resolving the most common disagreements in marriage / Tim and Joy Downs.
        p. cm.
    Includes bibliographical references.
    ISBN 0-8024-1423-0
    1. Marriage—Religious aspects—Christianity. 2. Conflict management—Religious aspects—Christianity. I. Downs, Joy. II. Title.

BV835 .D69 2003
248.8'44—dc21

2002014132

3 5 7 9 10 8 6 4

Printed in the United States of America

For Joy's parents, Bill and Laura Burns
Thank you for demonstrating a love for God,
for each other, and for your family for almost half a century.
Thank you for being a model to us
in your commitment to cling to each other
through happy and difficult times.
You have made our lives more secure and joyful,
and we love and respect you both.

To our precious children, Tommy, Erin, and Kelsey
Though we do not know who your mates will be,
we pray that God will give each of you
a husband or wife devoted to Him and to you.
It is our prayer that each of you will strive to please God
and stay committed to your mate
as you learn how to love your partner for better and for worse.
We love you more than we can ever say.

contents

Part Three: Resolving the Seven Conflicts

acknowledgments

thanks to our dear friends and family who prayed for us and shared the stories of their own marriages: Tom and Linda Barrett, Mark and Julie Bontrager, Dan and Julie Brenton, Ben and Janet Burns, Bill and Laura Burns, Bobby and Ann Clampett, Doug and Patty Daily, Mark and Erin Donalson, Steve and Myra Ellis, Jon and Nancy Fugler, Doug and Terri Haigh, Bill and Rese Hood, Jim and Renee Keller, Kent and Kim Kramer, Glenn and Beth Melhorn, Al and Diane Meyer, Tim and Noreen Muehlhoff, Mike and Renee Seay, Dave and Sande Sunde, Sam and Carol Thomsen, J. T. and Enid Walker, and John and Susan Yates. We appreciate all of your labor on our behalf and the encouragement that fueled our writing!

Thanks to our good friend Tim Muehlhoff for reading our manuscript as it progressed and offering a critical eye.

Thanks to our editor, Cheryl Dunlop, for her insights, corrections, and contributions to the text.

Thanks to our agent, Kathryn Helmers, for her sound guidance, wise counsel, and constant encouragement.

And a special thanks to the hundreds of couples who shared their struggles with us at FamilyLife Weekend to Remember Conferences. We hope this book gives something back to each of you.

part one

*Different People,
Different Dreams*

INTRODUCTIONS

my name is Tim Downs. I'd like you to meet my wife, Joy.

Joy and I want you to know that we wrote this book together—the two of us, husband and wife—drawing equally from both of our perspectives, share and share alike.

But I'm writing the introduction so I can get my side in first.

The decision to marry is something like two people climbing opposite sides of a mountain. They're both aiming for the same summit, but the experience of climbing can be very different for each of them. Joy and I were married in 1981 after a somewhat one-sided relationship. My side of the mountain was an easy climb, a smooth and gradual rise toward a simple decision. Her ascent was a tad steeper, more like an assault on Mount Everest without oxygen. But in the autumn of 1980 I finally proposed, and Joy, dazed and disoriented by the altitude, said yes.

We were advised to take part in premarital counseling at our local church—something I considered about as necessary as selecting the perfect china pattern. After all, we were going to be *married*. I asked Joy to spend the rest of her life with me and she said yes. If that isn't the ultimate test of compatibility, what is? Besides, we had just climbed an entire *mountain*. At last we were on top of the world, and I was in no mood to hear that this hard-earned summit might be only the first peak in an entire mountain range ahead.

The pastor began by informing us that he was leaving immediately to work at another church—probably because of couples like us, though he was kind enough not to say so. He had time for only one session, take it or leave it, a sort of "Jiffy Lube" version of premarital counseling. The pastor handed each of us a lengthy survey, a kind of personality inventory designed to evaluate our communication styles, our role preferences, our financial attitudes, and a host of other bothersome and insignificant issues. Our answers were tallied, and the results were transferred to a neat little chart—one for her, one for me—to illustrate in graphic form potential areas of incompatibility between us.

Joy's chart looked something like a lightning bolt, a jagged red line streaking down from left to right. My chart looked like a lightning bolt, too—but mine streaked down from the opposite direction. When her line shifted left, mine moved right; when her line rose, mine fell. In fact, our two charts were opposite in every way. According to the survey, I seemed to be a virtual mirror image of my bride-to-be.

The survey said that Joy was a people person, while I preferred to work and play alone. Joy liked to budget and save; I had no savings and only two items on my budget, eating out and video rentals. She was a principle-oriented person, whose first question was always, "What is the right thing to do?" I was a pragmatist who always asked, "What do I have to do to make this go away?" She felt things first and thought about them later. I thought first, and never got around to feeling much of anything at all. She said "tomayto," I said "tomahto" . . . and so it went.

At first, I thought it was all a mistake. How could two people be so opposite and still be so much in love? I tried flipping the page with my chart upside down and holding it up to the light. *That's* better—a perfect match! If only it were that easy. I wonder how many times in the years since then my wife has wished she could just flip *me* upside down?

The survey was trying to warn us that we were *different*, and that our differences went way beyond simple tastes or preferences. We were different in *fundamental* ways, ways that would not quickly surrender or pass into memory along with the other minor first-year adjustments of marriage. Our differences were there to stay, and they would become the source of many a "discussion" in the years ahead. As Joy likes to put it, "They tried to warn us that there were red flags, and we've been waving them at each other ever since." Of course, *I* wouldn't put it that way.

I tell you this story to make a point. I want to assure you that the authors of this book know something about conflict.

Not just the academic *theory* of conflict, or the sterile statistical *analysis* of conflict, but real *conflict*—genuine, day-to-day, what-galaxy-are-you-from/were-you-dropped-on-your-head-as-a-child conflict.

Joy and I have now been married for twenty-two years—but then, we have never believed that a marriage should be measured in years, any more than an adventure should be measured in miles. Ralph Waldo Emerson once wrote, "We ask for long life, but it's *deep* life or *noble* moments that signify. Let the measure of time be spiritual, not mechanical." Time, he said, can't be adequately measured by minutes and seconds alone, but by the quality of the events that fill it. So it is with marriage. Don't tell me how *long* you've been married; tell me what your marriage has been *through*.

Joy and I have been married for three children, two pets, one apartment, three houses, and one cross-country exodus. We have been together for three years of chemotherapy, the death of a mother and father, and the loss of several friends who can never be replaced. We have shared three MRIs, two CAT scans, one major surgery, and a host of other lumps, lacerations, and fractures. We have been together for public school, private school, and home school; for a change of career, a midlife crisis, and ongoing financial concerns; for infants and teenagers, diapers and prom dresses, kindergarten and college. . . .

That's how long we've been married.

When we were dating, Joy and I seemed to naturally agree about *everything*. We both liked triple-layer lasagna, shoulder rubs, golden retriever puppies, long autumn walks, and white-chocolate-chip cookies. We agreed about *all* the critical issues of life. Then marriage came along, and we found ourselves enrolled in a slightly more accelerated curriculum. Marriage is where life gets *serious*.

And through it all, our differences were always there. They never went away, not for a single day. They never said, "Hey, this is a really tough situation; let's quiet down for a while and let them work this out." No, it was in the really tough situations that they sometimes spoke the loudest. Joy and I seem instinctively to see things in different ways. Joy sees things her way, and I see them the right way. I love my wife dearly, but the survey was right—we are different, and we always will be. That's the way it is for us.

That's the way it is for you, too.

And that's why we wrote this book—to tell you that you and your mate are different, that your deepest differences will not go away, and that you can have a great marriage anyway.

If your life is as busy as ours, it's a significant commitment of time and energy to read an entire book. That's why, before you go any farther, we thought we should tell you three things about this book, so you'll know what you're getting yourself into.

First, this is a *practical* book. If you're looking for a book on conflict resolution by someone who isn't married, or by a scholar who has only studied conflict in a laboratory, you've come to the wrong place. Personally, we don't believe you really know what conflict *is* until you get married. "I used to have six theories of parenting," a wise man once said. "Now I have six children, and no theories of parenting." We are not only students of conflict, but we also are veterans of conflict, and we'll give you more than theories—we'll tell you how things work in the real world. And if you're looking for a book by a couple who claims that, because of their system, they no longer *have* any conflict, you've hit another dead end. If your goal is to eliminate all conflict from your marriage, we can't help you. We believe that conflict is an inevitable part of *every* marriage. Although the *amount* of conflict in marriage can certainly be reduced, and the *experience* of conflict can be greatly improved, the basic message of this book is that some conflicts *will not go away*—but you can learn to understand them and deal with them in a way that will allow you to love your mate more than ever.

Second, this is a *spiritual* book. You'll find a number of references to biblical teachings on the subjects of communication, compassion, understanding, forgiveness, and more. We've included this perspective for a very practical reason. In a sense, the Bible is essentially a book about conflict resolution. It tells the story of the greatest conflict of all time, how God has successfully sought to resolve that conflict, and how we can do the same with one another. The recurring conflicts described in this book are no easy matter. They are the result of fundamental differences between us, and trying to unravel them can drive us to the limits of our own resources—if not our sanity. As Dirty Harry reminded us, "A man's *got* to know his limitations." When you reach your limits, that's a good time to ask for outside help. We've sought the best.

I'll bet Joy would *never* have thought of Dirty Harry.

Finally, this is an *honest* book. Joy and I get tired of books by people who seem to have risen above it all—people who have conquered all fear, banished all doubt, and overcome all

17

obstacles. *We are not those people.* We want you to know that we still have disagreements, and we expect that we always will. We'll tell you what's worked for us, what hasn't, and what we're still struggling with. We'll speak to you not as masters lecturing novices, but as students helping other students. That's all this book is—a kind of study group for people who want their marriage to be everything it can be. We're pleased and honored to include you in our study group.

When C. S. Lewis was working on his classic book *The Problem of Pain,* he once said, "I wish this toothache would go away so I could write another chapter on pain." That's the way we feel—we wish we could stop disagreeing so we could write another chapter on conflict. But C. S. Lewis's toothache did not instantly disappear, and our fundamental differences will not simply go away. Lewis had to try to understand pain in the presence of pain, and we have to learn to love one another with all our differences intact.

That's what this book is all about.

A Note from Tim:
For Husbands Who Didn't Plan on Reading This Book

Bad news. Your wife is reading a book on conflict resolution. You know—how to understand your mate better, how to disagree more agreeably—that sort of thing. You know what *that* means. That means "conflict" is about to become a topic of conversation at your house. It's going to casually come up when you're eating dinner, when you're driving the kids to the soccer game, and when you finally get to bed late at night and you turn out the lights and you're already semi-comatose.

At first it's going to be little comments like, "I read something interesting today," or "I've been reading a really interesting book. I think you'd enjoy it." Then the book itself is going to start mysteriously turning up on your nightstand, or in the bathroom on top of your *Sports Illustrated* with some relevant passage conveniently bookmarked with a square of toilet paper.

And if you just sit there like tree fungus and ignore all those subtle hints, let me tell you, it's not going to go well for you. I know what you're thinking—it isn't fair, is it? After all, *you're* not the one who bought the book. She went to the mall to look for a carpet steamer, and she came home with a book on conflict! Did anyone ask if *you* wanted a book on conflict? You've been reading Tom Clancy's latest novel, but you're not asking *her* to read it, are you? Go ahead and think those things —but if you actually *say* them, I can promise you, it's *really* not going to go well for you.

So I'm going to make it easy for you. In our book, my wife and I have included a handful of short summaries we call "Quick Takes"—just a page or two at a time that will give you the gist of what we're trying to get across. When your wife comes to a Quick Take, she's going to stop and ask you to read it. Think of it as the *Reader's Digest* condensed version, or as an executive book summary. You'll get the main ideas in just a page or two, and your wife will know that you're taking an interest in your marriage and that you care about the things she cares about. That's important, by the way—we talk about that in chapter 6.

We may also ask you to stop and think about something, or to take a little survey, or maybe even to take a few minutes and talk something over with your wife. So do it! I know you care about your marriage, and I know you'd like to improve your style of conflict. Maybe you just weren't thinking about doing it right *now*. I know that, so I've made it as easy for you as I can. And who knows? You may find yourself reading more of our book than you thought you would.

Your wife bought a book on conflict resolution, and she wants to share it with you. It's only natural—you've been a big part of every marital conflict she's ever had. If you'll agree to read our summaries—not dragging your feet, but with a positive attitude—you'll be reading what your wife is reading and thinking about the things she's thinking about. And when it's late at night and you've just turned out the light and your wife suddenly says, "I read today that men often try to avoid conflict," instead of saying, "I don't want to talk about it," you'll be able to say, "Yes, and I read that sometimes it's because of the way women approach men."

Is this a deal or what?

A Note from Joy:
For Wives Who Didn't Plan on Reading This Book

Ladies, we do have some differences as husbands and wives, don't we? This fact was made very clear to me one day as I was listening to a Christian radio station. The DJs were taking a survey of husbands and wives in which they asked each of them what their greatest wish would be. The majority of the wives responded that they wanted to have a better and deeper marriage. The consensus of the husbands was that they wanted a better golf score! Is it any wonder that it's hard for us to be on the same page at the same time?

It's my guess that reading about marital conflict is not new to you. You've probably read about it, listened to tapes or radio programs, or watched something about it on TV. It's not news to you that you have conflict in your marriage, and I'll bet you've brought up the need for some changes in this area before—perhaps *many* times before. Maybe your husband just never thought it was necessary to do anything about it—until now. He may be reading this book because he finally understands that unresolved conflict has caused your marriage to grow cold and left you discouraged and maybe even without hope that anything can be different.

You are not alone. It's usually women who know that something is wrong with the relationship and that they need some help long before their husbands really see that there is a problem. Unfortunately, by the time the men are ready to take action, our hearts have become distant and hard. We grow tired of trying to spark some interest in them, and we give up.

Even if you're feeling hurt and angry, even if you feel like *throwing* this book at him rather than *reading* it, let me encourage you to give it a try. If your husband is reading this book, if he's showing an interest in making your marriage better and is willing to work on it, don't let your hurt or pride stand in the way. It has been said that "regret for the things we did can be tempered by time; it is regret for the things we did not do that is inconsolable." God will be merciful and forgiving for both the things we did and did not do, but there are still consequences for those things. A broken or lifeless marriage is too high a price for you to pay for not trying to repair the hurt in your relationship.

If you're a little reluctant to read this entire book, you can start with the short summaries we call "Quick Takes"—just a page or two at a time that will give you the gist of what we're trying to say. These short summaries may give you and your husband a springboard to begin to talk about these things. There are also inventories and questions to help you talk together about the roots, not just the symptoms, of some of the conflicts that never seem to go away. We'll also show you how to talk together in a way that will help you understand each other and feel heard, not just tolerated.

Take advantage of your husband's interest in improving your marriage even if the timing is not what you had wanted. You may feel discouraged or even hopeless, but remember what Luke told us: "Nothing will be impossible with God" (Luke 1:37).

CHapter one

the four stages of marital conflict

Several years ago we spoke at a weekend marriage conference in Cincinnati. It was Friday night, the conference was about to begin, and several hundred people had gathered in the Hyatt Regency ballroom. I (Tim) decided to kick off the weekend with a personal touch.

"I'd like to find the couple here tonight who has been married the longest," I said. "Not the couple who *feels* like they've been married the longest—the couple who has actually logged the most miles. Any volunteers?"

Older couples glanced about the ballroom, assessing their chances, and then hands began to slowly rise. Thirty-two years over on the left, thirty-five years back by the doorway, thirty-seven years right in the middle of the ballroom . . .

The winners were a couple sitting right in the front row. Because they were so accessible, I decided to ask them to come up on the platform with me for a little impromptu interview. As the audience applauded, they worked their way up to the podium and stood beside me, the woman to my left, her husband beside her.

"First of all," I began, "exactly how long have you been married?" I held out the microphone to the husband.

"Forty-seven years," he beamed. The audience erupted in

applause. As I was taking the microphone away I felt an icy hand seize my wrist. The woman pulled the microphone in front of her.

"Forty-*eight* years," she said as she glared at her husband. "We were married in 1939! You never *can* remember that!"

Now the man took the microphone again.

"Forty-*seven* years," he said defiantly, "and it *hasn't* been *easy!*"

Conflict is a part of every marriage, whether you've been married seven years or forty-seven. It can be a major source of anger, discouragement, and regret—but it doesn't have to be. When couples learn to handle conflict correctly, they are able to put their disagreements behind them, one at a time, as they are resolved. Like last year's scrapes and bruises, they were once painful but now almost forgotten. For these couples, past conflicts are nothing more than a part of their marital history, and their history is powerless to harm them.

It's the *present* that can destroy you.

Imagine a world where people can be injured, but no one can heal. A broken arm would require a splint forever; a wound would fester and seep for a lifetime. A bruise would never disappear, a scrape would be a constant annoyance, and a toothache would never cease. Imagine the lengths to which people would go in such a world to avoid injury. Imagine the premium that would be placed on beauty and the penalty that would be assigned for injuring another person. But most of all, *imagine the pain that people would live with every day of their lives.*

This is not an imaginary world; it is inhabited by those who never learn to handle conflict constructively. Their conflicts never become history. Like seeping wounds, their disagreements are always a part of the present. Every unresolved argument is a sore that never heals—a constant source of friction and annoyance— and every new disagreement is exacerbated by the last. Imagine the pain these people must live with every day of their lives. Imagine the lengths to which they would go to avoid conflict.

When couples fail to resolve their disagreements constructively, their attitude toward conflict tends to evolve through
four distinct stages over the course of the marriage.

Have It Your Way

She: *Honey, may I ask a small favor?*

He: *Of course, Darling, anything for you.*

She: *Would you mind very much changing your entire
personality for me?*

He: *It's the least I can do.*

Couples who are just married tend to settle arguments
quickly by simply deferring to each other. There is great motivation early on to avoid awkward confrontations that seem to
drain the romance from the new relationship. Newly married
couples find romance and conflict to be mutually exclusive, and
so the operating principle at this stage is "Have it your way"—
whatever it takes to preserve peace between us.

But after just a year or two of marriage, couples begin to
tire of endlessly *giving in.* They begin to realize that their partner's aggravating personal habits and annoying personality
quirks really *matter.* They still want peace—but they slowly
realize that there is such a thing as "peace at too great a price,"
and they enter the second phase of marital conflict.

Have It My Way

He: *Would you mind not doing that?*

She: *What?*

He: *That thing you do with your nails. You click your
nails.*

She: *You never mentioned it before.*

He: *Well, I'm mentioning it now. It bugs me.*

With this revelation, *her* mind begins to open to the possibilities. "If we're going to start mentioning things that *bother* us," she reasons, "I've got a few hundred things that I could mention too." She may actually say this out loud, which is then the beginning of an entire evening's entertainment.

In the second phase of marital conflict, couples tend to swing to the other extreme. They begin to assert their own needs and wants, reasoning that the problem all along has been their silence. They begin to feel that they are being taken advantage of. While she has been deferring, he has been getting his own way—and he, of course, feels exactly the same way about her. Now they begin to give voice to a whole series of preferences that have become increasingly clear to them after two years of life in Pleasantville. "I *don't* like this, I *do* want that . . ."

But the second phase is exhausting, and after realizing that they'll get nowhere by endlessly butting heads, the couple attempts to bargain and compromise. That's the third phase.

Have It Our Way

She: *I thought you were going to start picking up your own clothes.*

He: *I thought you were going to start putting gas in the car. You left it on empty. Again.*

She: *I'll get gas if you pick up your clothes.*

He: *(Pauses) Who goes first?*

She: *We'll both go on "three." Ready?*

The third phase is a stage of compromise and negotiation, when couples begin to realize that if they can just put their heads together instead of *banging* them together, they might be able to work out their differences. And so the negotiations begin. They confront each disagreement with eagerness and enthusiasm. They listen, they discuss, and they compromise, over and over again—over and over and over *again*. Then one day the eagerness and enthusiasm begin to fade.

In the third phase couples begin to face more and more of the difficult issues of life together: in-law relationships, job pressures, increasing time demands, financial struggles, parenting decisions. . . . There's more and more to disagree *about* —and disagree they do. Now conflicts seem to bombard them from all sides. There just isn't *time* to discuss them all, and even when there's time, there isn't enough energy. They begin to feel as if they are furiously bailing out a sinking boat, but the water continues to rise. They differ on all kinds of issues, and the sheer number of differences may cause them to begin to question how compatible they really are.

They're ready for the fourth and final phase . . .

Have It Any Way You Want

She: Can I talk to you about something?

He: What is it now?

She: I think you need to spend more time with the kids.

He: Fine.

She: Fine? You mean you will?

He: Okay. Sure. Whatever.

For those who fail to resolve conflict constructively, the fourth phase is a period of resignation. Exhausted by the energy crisis of daily life and hopeless over the backlog of unresolved issues waiting to be discussed, they become pacifists. *Have it any way you want. What's the point in fighting about it?*

By this time the couple has negotiated and compromised on an exhausting number of minor preferences and desires. But a handful of stubborn disagreements still remains, and these issues seem to crop up again and again with discouraging regularity. Like ancient Rome, all roads lead to them. No matter what topic *begins* the disagreement, sooner or later the partners find themselves on familiar ground. "Oh no, not *this* again!" We call these unsolvable issues the Seven Conflicts of marriage.

The Seven Conflicts are a reality for all married couples, and they are a source of ongoing frustration and discouragement. Their very *existence* is annoying. Couples feel they should have resolved these differences by this time, and their failure to do so must mean something is wrong between them. Not at all.

Psychologist John Gottman is a relationship expert who has studied the conflict styles of married couples for many years. He believes that all marital conflicts fall into one of two categories. "Either they can be resolved," he writes, "or they are perpetual, which means they will be a part of your lives forever, in some form or another."[1] Gottman estimates that almost 70 percent of marital conflicts are *perpetual*. "The majority of marital problems fall into this category—69 percent, to be exact. Time and again when we do four-year follow-ups of couples, we find that they are still arguing about precisely the same issue. It's as if four minutes have passed rather than four years."[2]

If Gottman is correct, only three out of ten marital disagreements will have a tidy solution. The rest, like an alien shape-shifter, will return to visit us again and again in some unexpected form.

Couples in the fourth stage often wonder if these unresolved issues reveal some secret weakness in their partner. Each begins to suspect the other of immaturity, pride, or sheer pigheadedness. They know that when the subject inevitably shifts to one of *those* topics, there will be no resolution. They will end up, as always, in an angry stalemate, burying the disagreement like toxic waste until it surfaces again another day.

How do the Seven Conflicts develop? Our first disagreements in marriage are over relatively minor issues; later, they are over more significant ones; after several years we have whittled down our areas of disagreement to the ones that *really* matter to us. They are far more than opinions or even values— they are a part of the way we see the world itself. Over the years, as we express our differences and resolve them, we engage in a kind of pruning process: First we cut away twigs, then branches, then limbs, until we finally come to the trunk of the tree itself.

The Seven Conflicts are the result of fundamental convictions all of us possess about how life and love and marriage *ought* to work. They tell us what's good and bad, right and wrong, fair and unjust. They are the operating system of our computer; they are behind the scenes, invisible, but always running in the background. They are the result of gender differences, environmental influences, and individual temperament—but regardless of the source, by the time we are adults, they are so intimate a part of us that we are no more aware of them than we are the color of our own eyes.

And that's the problem. We all assume that we are marrying someone just like us, with similar opinions and values and tastes, unaware that far below the surface there may reside a worldview that differs from our own at significant points—and these differences will ultimately surface in the form of the Seven Conflicts. Each of these arguments represents a clash of worldviews, and each disagreement appears impossible to resolve because it seems inconceivable to consider the issue from any other perspective than the one we *know* to be correct. Like the spot where the retina attaches to the optic nerve, there are no receptor cells at all; the Seven Conflicts represent our most persistent blind spots.

When we lose hope of ever really *resolving* our deepest differences, the Seven Conflicts become the "no-man's-land" of marriage. We're forced to constantly check ourselves: *Don't go there.* We begin to fence off areas of the relationship where no one dares to tread—but we do this at a great price. The benefit of this approach is peace, or at least the absence of conflict, but the price of this evasion is the very thing we want most from marriage—true intimacy.

The fourth stage of marital conflict is the final stage, and it has been recognized by students of the human condition for thousands of years. In the book of Proverbs, collected three millennia ago, Solomon characterized the fourth stage this way: "It is better to live in a corner of the roof than in a house shared with a contentious woman" (25:24). Better to live in the attic, he said, than to have to endure endless conflict.

Many couples who begin marriage with perfectly lovely homes end up spending much of their lives in a cold, dark attic. They don't have to. It's a short distance back from the attic to the family room—and even the bedroom—once they learn to recognize and anticipate the seven fundamental issues that divide us all.

CHAPTER TWO

I Have a Dream

Tim: *I grew up in a time not that long ago but in a world that no longer exists. I remember a white split-level home in suburban St. Louis on an acre and a half of zoysia as soft as a down comforter. I remember a mother who lived to serve her family and a father who was strict and severe but emotionally absent. I remember walking to school, coming home without homework, and simply telling my mother, "I'm going out." Out where? "To play." I rode my bike on busy streets without a helmet, wore PF Flyers that cost $9.95 a pair, and carried an Uncle Henry pocketknife wherever I went. What I loved most about my childhood is that I was free.*

Joy: *I grew up in Columbus, Ohio, in a neighborhood where every child belonged to every family. We spent every summer day together at the neighborhood pool, and through the year we all walked together to school and back. We walked home for lunch as well—we walked through the woods, through places I would never allow my children to walk today. But my parents never had to worry if I would make it home each day, because, above all, my neighborhood was safe.*

Tim: *There are things about my childhood I loved, and things I despised. There are parts of my early days that*

I long to reproduce in my own family, and things I'll do most anything to avoid. The irony is, I'm not always sure what those things are; they live invisibly inside me, lurking in the background, operating not as specific goals but as indefinable longings—as dreams. Like post-hypnotic suggestions, they inform all my conscious actions, though I'm seldom aware they even exist. As I grew up, I collected a series of fuzzy mental images of how my life would look one day. How it should look. I have a dream.

Joy: *When we got married, Tim naturally expected that his wife would share not only his tastes and opinions, but his dreams as well. What he never counted on is that I would have dreams of my own—very different dreams. This difference in our mental images, this disparity in our "shoulds" and "oughts," was what originally attracted us to each other. But in marriage, the same differences became the source of many of our disagreements. He had his dreams, and I had mine. It took us quite a while to understand that our biggest conflicts would come when we were both right.*

The Battle of Dreams

We all have dreams—mental images of how our lives are supposed to look and feel. Marital researcher Scott Stanley calls these unconscious longings *hidden issues.* "Hidden issues," he writes, "are the deeper, fundamental issues that usually lie underneath the arguments about issues and events. . . . For all too many couples, the hidden issues never come out. They fester and produce fear, sadness, and resentment that can erode and eventually destroy the marriage." The author's solution? "The most important thing you can do is simply to talk about these hidden issues constructively, perhaps at a time set aside just for this purpose."[1]

Easier said than done. The problem with hidden issues is precisely that—they're *hidden.* How do you find the Invisible Man? You blow smoke at him and look for the hole he leaves behind, or shine a light on him and search for his shadow. You don't discover his presence directly; you only become aware of him through something he *affects.* A hidden issue is almost impossible to spot until something comes along to define its contours.

That "something" is usually conflict.

Christians are inadvertently taught to fear conflict. The apostle Peter once told us, "All of you be harmonious, sympathetic, brotherly, kindhearted, and humble in spirit" (1 Peter 3:8). Paul admonished Christians to be "like-minded, having the same love, being one in spirit and purpose" (Philippians 2:2 NIV). Doesn't it follow, then, that the ideal marriage is one that lacks conflict of any kind?

The simplest conflicts are the disagreements where one of you is just plain *wrong.* You got the facts wrong, or you forgot, or—to be honest—you just didn't care. Though we sometimes fight even when we know we're wrong, our better side usually gets the best of us and sooner or later we own up to it. *Sorry about that. I was wrong, you were right.*

The more difficult arguments—the ones that make up the Seven Conflicts—are the ones in which you're *both* right. These disagreements are harder to resolve because neither one of you wants to let go. But then, neither one of you should. At its worst, conflict is when you demonstrate your selfishness, arrogance, and sheer mule-headedness. But at its best, *conflict is when you fight for what you really believe in.*

Throughout our married life, we have often disagreed in our approach to raising our kids. Joy thinks our son should wear his bicycle helmet to simply ride around the block; Tim thinks it's an unnecessary nuisance for such a short distance. Joy thinks we should remind the kids each time they go out to take a jacket; Tim thinks they should learn to remember for

33

themselves, and a little frostbite just might do the trick. Joy thinks we should install Internet filtering software on our home computer to protect the kids from accidentally going to inappropriate sites; Tim thinks the kids should know that the sites are there, but develop the self-control not to visit them. At times, we seemed to disagree about *everything*.

Over time, we began to recognize the outline of the Invisible Man. We realized that all of the individual disagreements were just like the leaves on a tree, obscuring the trunk behind it. Our differences were all part of a *single disagreement*; when it came to the children, Joy instinctively placed their security above all else, and Tim instinctively valued their autonomy—their need to take risks in order to grow in confidence and capability.

What could possibly be wrong with valuing a child's security? What could be wrong with wanting to raise a child in such a way that she actually *survives* childhood?

And what could be wrong with valuing a child's autonomy? What could be wrong with teaching a child to take reasonable risks, to begin to prepare him for the time when he'll be making decisions on his own?

Of course, there's nothing wrong with *either* perspective. The problem is that each of us instinctively approaches all child-rearing decisions from our own perspective—the *right* perspective. Neither of us could explain exactly *why* our perspective is right—but then, why should we have to? Isn't it obvious?

Joy's perspective is much more than her opinion; it's her *dream*. Joy's fuzzy mental image is a photograph of children who are first of all safe and warm, sheltered from the elements, protected from all the very real dangers that threaten children today. That's an excellent dream.

But Tim's dream is of children who are first of all *free*, risk takers who think for themselves, take responsibility for their own lives, and bounce back quickly from adversity. That's a good dream too.

They're *both* good dreams, but how in the world do you

combine them? When one partner wants to push the birds out of the nest, and the other wants to protect them from hitting the ground, what do you do?

There's an easy solution to our conflict—one of us could just give in. But what would be the implications for the kids if we completely neglected the value of security? Would we still *have* any children? And what would be the long-term impact on the kids if we ignored the value of autonomy, the goal of teaching them to stand on their own two feet? The problem is that we're *both* right.

It took years of lengthy "discussions" before we finally realized two critical things: that we were not really battling about bicycle helmets and jackets and computers at all, and that *we were on the same side.* We simply chose different paths to our common goal, a mature and thriving child.

The Seven Conflicts of Marriage

Once we recognized and understood the underlying cause of our disagreements, we began to search for others. Was it possible that there were *more* fundamental issues like this, more instinctive blind spots that were the root of other disagreements? Sure enough, others began to emerge, and after many more discussions we finally identified seven fundamental areas of disagreement.

We began to discuss our conclusions with other couples and ask if they had observed a similar phenomenon in their own marriages. We asked each couple, "Are there recurring areas of conflict in your marriage—areas that you seem to come back to over and over again? Are there topics that you *know* you'll disagree about?" In each case, we encouraged them to try to determine what they were *really* fighting about. To our surprise, we found that other couples had recurring disagreements over the very same seven issues.

Our next step was to test our theory with a larger audience. Over the next two years, as we traveled and spoke at marriage conferences across the nation, we began to take a survey of our audiences. We asked more than a thousand couples a series of questions about their experience with conflict, and in the process we made a remarkable discovery: Wherever we went, our findings were consistent. There seem to be seven common underlying issues that are the root cause of most of the conflict in married life: *Security, Loyalty, Responsibility, Caring, Order, Openness,* and *Connection.*

But what's the point in discussing all this? Aren't the Seven Conflicts what John Gottman described as "perpetual"? Because of our fundamental differences, aren't we doomed to repeat these disagreements over and over again in different forms? And if they won't go away, why bother to talk about them at all?

The reason we need to talk about the Seven Conflicts is precisely *because* they won't go away. They're always there, and they always *matter.* Each of the Seven Conflicts is much more than a difference of opinions; it's a battle of dreams—and dreams die hard. If you feel like having Italian food for dinner, but your mate prefers Chinese, you might be disappointed; but if you have a deep, pervasive longing to build a safe, secure home, and your mate is not cooperating, you'll be *much* more than disappointed. "Hope deferred makes the heart sick," Proverbs 13:12 tells us, and the Seven Conflicts are exactly that —deeply held hopes that are deferred or sometimes denied altogether by our partner, the very person we feel should most share our dreams. When these seven issues are simply avoided and left to fester, they produce the kind of sickness in a marriage that Proverbs warns us about, an underlying atmosphere of anger, bitterness, and resentment. No wonder Scott Stanley says, "Hidden issues often drive our most frustrating and destructive arguments."[2]

But if we *do* talk about them, since they're not going to just disappear, what can we really hope to accomplish? Perhaps the best way to answer this question is by telling you what understanding the Seven Conflicts did for *us.*

36

First, understanding the Seven Conflicts helped us to *identify our dreams*. Remember, dreams are often *hidden* issues. It would be very helpful in a marriage if a husband would simply say to his wife, "I should warn you that I'm extremely sensitive about issues of loyalty. It's a dream of mine to have a perfectly loyal wife." Unfortunately, he may be consciously unaware of his sensitivity altogether. But just wait until the first argument about the in-laws—*then* the dream will go to work, lurking in the background, fueling the anger and confusion and frustration. The problem is that this husband and wife may go on forever believing that they're fighting about the in-laws, never recognizing that the underlying concern is really all about *Loyalty*. Identifying the Seven Conflicts allowed us to ignore the diversion created by a hundred minor disagreements and talk about the *real* issues. "What do you *long* for? What is your mental image of how marriage *ought* to be? What does a husband *look* like to you? How do you think kids *should* be raised? Tell me about your *dreams*."

Second, understanding the Seven Conflicts helped us to *put our differences in perspective*. When it came to rearing the kids, one moment we thought that we disagreed about *everything*, from allowances to curfews to appropriate forms of discipline. Suddenly we understood that we only disagreed about *one* thing, but that one issue influenced our approach to dozens of others. That understanding alone changed our self-perception, from a couple that never could seem to agree, to a couple with only a handful of fundamental differences. That change in perspective allowed us to focus on the disease rather than the symptoms. "For every thousand hacking at the leaves," Emerson wrote, "only one is striking at the root." It's an exhausting process to try to fell a tree one branch at a time. What a relief it was to be able to finally "strike at the root" and watch an entire tree come crashing to the ground.

Third, understanding the Seven Conflicts helped us to *understand each other's true motives*. Joy was concerned about the children's safety, but Tim didn't seem to care. Tim wanted the kids to grow to independence, but she seemed to want to keep them tied to her apron strings. The other's perspective seemed so selfish, so shortsighted, and that naturally produced anger in each of us. *Why don't you care what happens to the kids?* We both cared, of course; we both wanted the best for the kids, but that was hard to believe. Psychologists Clifford Notarius and Howard Markman call this problem *hot thoughts.* "All too often we tend to think the worst about our partner rather than the best," they write. "When you latch on to the worst possible explanations for your partner's behavior, you're going to make your partner *and* yourself feel miserable."[3] Understanding the underlying conflict allowed us to eliminate our "hot thoughts" by seeing the other's motives in a completely different light.

Fourth, understanding the Seven Conflicts helped us to *anticipate areas of conflict.* The problem with a minefield is that the dangers are buried, and so the explosions are always unexpected. We begin by discussing bicycle helmets, and before we know it, it's a full-fledged argument. How did *that* happen? Once we understood each other's underlying dreams, we could look for other issues that might be influenced by those desires. That allowed us to take a *proactive* approach to our differences rather than always having to clean up the messes and bandage the wounds after conflict. We knew where we were likely to disagree, and we could be ready for it.

Finally, understanding the Seven Conflicts helped us to *work together as partners* instead of battling as foes. Once we understood each other's dreams, once we each realized what the other person was valuing, our attitudes changed. We wanted to help fulfill the other's dreams rather than stubbornly defend our own turf. That change in attitude has allowed us to work together as partners instead of constantly shouting at each other from opposite sides of the fence.

Believing in Dreams Together

In the seven chapters that follow we'll describe each of the Seven Conflicts in detail. We'll illustrate each conflict from our own marriage, and we'll give some of the insights and ideas from the hundreds of couples who responded to our survey. We'll help you identify where you and your mate stand in relation to each issue—and, more important, where you stand in relation to each other.

Dreams die hard, but your dreams don't have to die at all. In the final eight chapters, we'll show you how to grow in love and intimacy even when your dreams are different. We'll help you identify the approaches to conflict that don't work for you and replace them with strategies that will. We'll give you five essential things to do before your next conflict begins, and we'll show you how to speak to your mate in a way that will guarantee your words get the warmest possible reception. The goal of *The Seven Conflicts* is to help you experience the same five benefits we described above: to identify your own dreams, to understand your mate's true motives, to put your differences in perspective, to anticipate areas of disagreement, and to learn to work together as partners.

The presence of conflict in your marriage is not a condemnation. It simply means that you have *dreams*—that you are human beings and that there are things you long for, things you truly believe in. The question is, how will you believe in them *together*? How will you honor each other's dreams, even when they sometimes conflict? You know what to do when one of you is wrong; what will you do when you both think you're right? How will you deal with the Seven Conflicts of marriage?

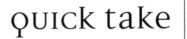

QUICK take

For Chapters 1 and 2

If you have disagreements in your marriage, you're not alone. Conflict is a part of every marriage, and it can be a major source of anger, discouragement, and regret—but it doesn't have to be. When couples learn to handle conflict correctly, they are able to put their disagreements behind them. But when couples fail to resolve their disagreements constructively, their attitude toward conflict tends to evolve through four distinct stages over the course of the marriage.

When we're first married our attitude is "Have it your way." Couples who are newly married settle conflicts quickly by simply giving in. But after two or three years, our attitude shifts to "Have it my way." Here we swing to the other extreme and begin to assert our own needs and wants. When we begin to tire of constantly butting heads, we move to the third stage, "Have it our way." In this stage we do our best to compromise and work through all our differences—until we realize it's an endless and exhausting process, and then we move to the final stage, "Have it any way you want." This final stage is a period of resignation where we begin to dread and avoid all conflict.

The truth is, almost 70 percent of our conflicts are *perpetual.* These disagreements return to visit us again and again in different forms because we fail to recognize the underlying issues that fuel them. All of us have fundamental convictions about how life and love and marriage *ought* to work, and these convictions are so instinctive to us that we're no more aware of them than we are the color of our own eyes. These basic differences in worldview fall into seven categories, and they're behind most of our disagreements in daily life. We call these seven fundamental issues the Seven Conflicts of marriage.

The simplest conflicts are the disagreements where one of you is just plain wrong. The more difficult arguments—the ones that make up the Seven Conflicts—are the ones where you're *both* right. At its worst, conflict is when you demonstrate your selfishness, arrogance, and sheer muleheadedness. But at its best, conflict is when you fight for what you really believe in.

We often disagreed about raising our children. At times it seemed that we disagreed about everything, but then we began to realize that our disagreements all stemmed from a single difference in worldview. When it came to the children, Joy instinctively placed their security above all else, and Tim instinctively valued their autonomy. What could possibly be wrong with valuing a child's security? What could be wrong with wanting to raise a child in such a way that she actually *survives* childhood?

And what could be wrong with valuing a child's autonomy? What could be wrong with preparing a child for the time when he'll be making decisions on his own?

Of course, there's nothing wrong with *either* perspective. The problem is that each of us instinctively approached all child-rearing decisions from our own perspective—the *right* perspective. Neither of us could explain exactly *why* our perspective was right—but then, why should we have to? Isn't it obvious?

We call these deeply held perspectives *dreams*, and dreams die hard. We could have easily resolved our disagreements; one of us could have just given in. But which one? The problem is, we were both right.

Once we understood the underlying cause of our disagreements about the children, we began to search for more. Was it possible that our *other* disagreements could be traced to underlying issues? Sure enough, other issues began to emerge.

We began to discuss our conclusions with other couples and to ask if they had observed a similar phenomenon in their own marriages. To our surprise, we found that other couples had recurring disagreements over the very same concerns. Over the next two years, as we traveled and spoke at marriage conferences across the nation, we began to take a survey with our audiences. We asked more than a thousand couples a series of questions about their own experience with conflict. By the time we were finished, we had identified seven common underlying issues that are the root cause of most of the conflicts in married life: *Security, Loyalty, Responsibility, Caring, Order, Openness,* and *Connection.*

What's the point in discussing these issues if they won't go away? We discovered five benefits. Understanding the Seven Conflicts helped us to identify our dreams, put our differences in perspective, understand each other's true motives, anticipate areas of conflict, and work together as partners instead of battling as foes.

In the chapters that follow we describe each of the Seven Conflicts in detail. We illustrate each conflict from our own relationship and from the marriages of other couples. We help you identify where you and your mate stand in relation to each issue—and, more important, where you stand in relation to each other. You can find all this in the next seven chapters, or you can read about it in the Quick Take that follows chapter 9.

part two

The Seven Conflicts
of Marriage

CHAPTER THREE

Protection and Provision

Tim: *The year was 1985, and our son Tommy had just learned to ride a bicycle without training wheels at the glorious age of three.*

Joy: *I was proud of him, too, but it was a little unnerving for me.*

Tim: *To see my son racing off down the sidewalk at only three was a real thrill for me. It was a part of my dream—kids who were free to go where they want, when they want. As I said in the last chapter, I grew up with a lot of freedom myself.*

Joy: *Sure, Tim had a lot of freedom, but what he's not telling you is that he's only alive today because of the sheer grace of God. Tim gives you a Beaver Cleaver picture of his childhood, as if all his freedom meant was that he rode carefree around his neighborhood with the wind whistling through his flattop. Not so. Did he mention that he once set his pants on fire by mounting model rockets to his handlebars?*

Tim: *The Green Hornet used to have those. It was very cool.*

Joy: *I imagine all the moms grabbing their children when Tim went riding by, scrambling into the house, and bolting all the shutters. He had more visits to the emergency*

> *room in his first six years of life than Tim "The Tool Man" Taylor ever did.*

Tim: *It was mostly for head injuries. Believe me, Joy's gotten a lot of mileage out of that.*

Joy: *Tim once burned down two of his father's prize evergreens in their front yard. He once shot a hole in his father's shoulder with a bottle rocket gone awry.*

Tim: *Now that you mention it, Dad did seem to be angry a lot.*

Joy: *I could write pages. When I grew up in Ohio, I had a mother who always knew where I was going and with whom I'd be playing. Is it any wonder that with Tim's history of freedom and independence, I would value security more than he does? I didn't go through twenty-one hours of labor with Tommy just to have him perish in his first adventure with his dad.*

The Two Sides of Security

In your own marriage, one of you will instinctively place a higher value on *Security*. Security is the need to be safe, the desire to know that you and yours are first of all protected from harm. Several responses from our survey revealed a desire for Security . . .

- *I like to spend, and she likes to save.*

- *When we have a major purchase, he wants to buy new and the most expensive quality. I would prefer to spend less but still get the job done.*

- *I want to feel secure—in his love, in my home, in our marriage, with him versus his family, financially—and I would like him to lead us spiritually (I long for this).*

- *Why does he feel the need to spend the extra money we have instead of saving it?*

- *I always wait until he's in bed and then I double-check the door, because sometimes he forgets to lock it.*

- *Why am I always the one who tucks the kids in at night?*

- *Why does he have to save everything? Why can't he throw anything away?*

Dangers come in many forms—physical and emotional, real and imagined—and so the dream of Security is a tree that puts out many branches. There are two chief offshoots from this tree: the desire for *Protection* and the desire for *Provision*.

Protection: Safety First

Protection in its most basic form is the instinct for survival, but it covers a lot more. Protection also includes the longing for safety, stability, and even comfort. Commercials that are aired at Christmastime show images of families snuggled together around the fireplace, images of warmth and love and Security. A protected family is one that has everything it needs to be safe, warm, dry, and happy.

Provision: Preparing for Future Needs

Provision is the desire to make sure everyone has enough, a desire that makes it necessary to both collect and save. Provision is concerned not only about the present but the future. Sure, we have enough *now*—but what about tomorrow? "Look at an ant," Proverbs advises us. "Watch it closely; let it teach you a thing or two. Nobody has to tell it what to do. All summer it stores up food; at harvest it stockpiles provisions" (6:6–8 THE MESSAGE). If you value Security, this may be your life verse.

Because Security looks to the future, it would rather save than spend. "Do we have to spend that much? It would be nice —but if we spend it today, we won't have it tomorrow."

Because Security wants to provide, it would rather collect than throw away. "I know we no longer need this, but what if we get rid of it and then we need it again? If we save it, we *have* it, and it'll be there just in case."

Because Security wants to protect, it has an aversion to risk. "Why do you want to try that? There are a lot safer things we can do that are just as fun." It isn't that the one who dreams of Security doesn't want to have fun—it's just that she's valuing something more. The Seven Conflicts aren't simply issues of preference; they're matters of *priority*. A dream is a non-negotiable, an essential priority. She's willing to take risks, to seek adventure, and to seize the day—as long as everyone is safe. Security comes *first*.

By the way, in case you're getting the wrong idea here, the dream of Security isn't gender specific. We don't mean to suggest that men are always the risk takers while women are always seeking to Protect and Provide. Our dreams are influenced by our family of origin, our built-in temperament, and the culture around us. Men who were born in the Great Depression era are often far more security oriented than men *and* women of later generations. If your childhood home was unstable, you may have an increased desire for Security as an adult. If your childhood home was especially warm and secure, you may long to reproduce that environment in your own home. It's difficult, if not impossible, to ascribe our deepest longings to a single cause. The point here is that either one of you may have the dream of Security.

But there is one variable that tends to tip the scale of Security toward women—the arrival of children. As Joy said earlier, "I didn't go through twenty-one hours of labor with Tommy just to have him perish in his first adventure with his dad." Women have a greater original investment in children, and they often sense that the greater burden of the children's Security continues to be theirs. Marriage is where life gets serious —but parenting is where life gets *critical*. Children are like a lens that focuses and magnifies the fears and longings of parents. We value our own Security, but we can get *frantic* about our children's safety. We may have only a minor desire for Security as a single person or as a young married, but when children come along, we sometimes find that our minor desire has blossomed into a full-blown *passion*.

Differing Priorities

Security often requires you to limit your freedom in some way—and that's how the argument begins. If Protection and Provision are not your natural priorities, then your Security-minded partner can seem like a killjoy. Why can't he lighten up? Why can't he stop worrying about everything? You have to take *some* risks, or what's the point of being alive?

But if Security is your priority, then your risk-taking partner seems just plain irresponsible. After all, it's *safety* we're talking about here, and surely that comes before everything else. Fun is good, risk is good, but let's not get carried away. We are *responsible* here. Let's not enjoy today at tomorrow's expense.

When you discuss these issues in your own marriage—and you undoubtedly do—you may have never realized that it's Security you've been discussing all along. That's because the Seven Conflicts are *hidden* issues, remember? We fail to recognize the Security issue as such because it comes to us in the form of a dozen smaller, seemingly unrelated arguments. They don't look like conflicts about Security—they look like arguments about money and irresponsibility and overprotecting the kids. The goal is to look behind the *apparent* disagreement and ask, "What are we *really* fighting about here?"

Let's observe a few disagreements from the marriages of couples we've interviewed and see if you can spot the root of Security underneath.

He: Isn't this a great vacation?
She: Yeah. Great.

49

He: *How did you like the parasailing? Wasn't that incredible?*

She: *Uh huh. How much did that cost, anyway?*

He: *Only forty bucks.*

She: *Each?*

He: *It was worth it. Where do you want to go for dinner tonight?*

She: *I was thinking maybe I could cook tonight. There's a little kitchenette in the room . . .*

He: *What's your problem, anyway?*

She: *What problem?*

He: *I went all out to plan this vacation—first-class air-fare, beachfront hotel room, four-star restaurants—and all you do is drag your feet.*

She: *Does everything have to be so . . . expensive?*

He: *There you go again! You never want to have fun anymore.*

The husband in the scenario above thinks they're disagreeing about their approaches to fun. He fears that his wife no longer wants to be his recreational partner, something that's very important to him. *She's no fun anymore. . . . Maybe she's getting older. Maybe she's just getting dull! Before long all she'll want to do is lie around the house and watch TV.*

He might also conclude that they're fighting about money. *All she wants to do is hoard money! What's the point in saving money if you never get a chance to spend any of it? We're not going to be young forever. By the time she's ready to spend some money, we'll be too old to enjoy it.*

But they aren't disagreeing about having fun, and they're not disagreeing about money. Those are just the *apparent* conflicts. Underneath it all, they're arguing about Security. She needs to know that this no-limits vacation won't put them in debt for the rest of their lives. She wants to enjoy the present, too, but not at the expense of the future—not at the expense of *Security.*

> *He:* *Look what I found in the trash can. Our toaster!*
> *She:* *It's our **old** toaster.*
> *He:* *You weren't going to throw it away, were you?*
> *She:* *Of course. We just bought a brand-new one.*
> *He:* *But it still works. Look, I'll plug it in . . . See?*
> *She:* *Why would we save the old toaster when we have a brand-new one? We don't need two toasters.*
> *He:* *What if the new one breaks? It's good to have a backup.*
> *She:* *Jack, our attic is **filled** with "backups."*
> *He:* *Why would you throw away a perfectly good toaster?*
> *She:* *If it was "perfectly good," why in the world did we buy a **new** one?*
> *He:* *I just don't like to waste things. I guess **my** family didn't have money to burn like **yours** did.*

The husband's desire to save a worn-out toaster even after they've bought a new one seems downright irrational to his wife—and he has a hard time explaining it himself. He tries to offer a logical rationale—the need for a backup, the moral responsibility not to be wasteful—but deep inside, all he knows for sure is that it *feels* wrong. He doesn't want a toaster; he wants Security. If one toaster breaks, now they have another. They're *Protected.* Now they can *Provide,* even if it's only half-browned toast.

But the argument is about to get ugly. In his desperation to provide a rational explanation for his desire, he suggests that it's really all his *wife's* problem. His wife is *wasteful,* and, worse than that, she picked up the bad habit from her family. "The best defense is a good offense," the old saying goes, and this man has put it into practice. But he has forgotten another ancient piece of wisdom: "A gentle answer turns away wrath, but a harsh word stirs up anger" (Proverbs 15:1).

This couple couldn't see the forest for the trees, and now they may spend the rest of the evening arguing about anything *but* Security.

She: *Jimmy forgot his umbrella again.*

He: *You're kidding. Again?*

She: *Now I'm going to have to drop it off at his school.*

He: *Why?*

She: *Because it's supposed to rain this afternoon, that's why. I don't want him to get soaked to the bone on the way home.*

He: *Anne, we live a hundred yards from the bus stop.*

She: *It's far enough to get drenched. I don't want him to catch a cold.*

He: *Stop coddling him. Let him catch a cold; it's the only way he's going to learn to take his umbrella.*

She: *And when he catches a cold, who's going to take care of him all day? Not you, that's for sure. I swear, I don't think you'd put him out if he was on fire.*

Conflicts over Security can be difficult because, to both partners, the issue seems so *obvious*. To her, the argument boils down to: *I care about the kids' welfare and you don't.* For him, the bottom line is: *If you don't stop babying the kids, they'll never grow up.* Both have good goals in mind—good *dreams*—but they're approaching the situation from opposite sides. They see the flaws in their partner's position, but they're completely unaware of their own blind spots. *Why doesn't he care about Jimmy? Why won't she stop smothering him?*

To make matters worse, the husband just used a loaded word. "Stop *coddling* him," he said. The word means "to treat indulgently; to baby." His wife doesn't need a dictionary to know what it means—and she knows exactly what he's intending by it. In response, she suggests that his attitude is not only callous, but selfish, since she is the one who will have to take care of the sick child. It's easy to be the risk taker when you're not the one who has to pay the price for it.

This couple began by talking about a forgotten umbrella, but in less than one minute they arrived at the root of the conflict, the issue of Security. The argument is a familiar one, but they've never been able to give it a name. They disagree, but they're not really sure what they're disagreeing *about*.

She: *Here's one more bag. We need to put this in too.*

He: *Jane, we're only going away for three days. You've packed enough stuff to last us a month!*

She: *We've still got some room. You can squeeze it in over there.*

He: *That's not the point. (Pokes at the bag) What is all this stuff?*

She: *(Crossly) Things we need.*

He: *We can't possibly need all this. Just once I wish we would set a one-bag limit. One bag for each of us, and that's it.*

She: *And what would you do when you got there and you forgot something?*

He: *I'd just do without it. Or I'd go to the store and buy it.*

She: *You'd go to the store and buy things we already own. Now that makes sense. Stop making such a fuss over a few suitcases.*

He: *That's easy for you to say; you don't have to fit it all in the trunk.*

Every time they prepare for a trip, they end up in an argument. She overpacks—at least *he* thinks so. Each time a vacation approaches, he tells himself that *this* time he's just going to bite his lip and hold his tongue—but there always seems to be "one more bag" that sends him over the edge and sets the argument in motion.

He wants his wife to explain the need for "all this stuff." She is not about to have to justify every item she's packed. She wants to make sure that wherever they go and whatever circumstances arise, they will have everything they need. At this point, he would just as soon go naked and hungry.

He would have a hard time explaining why this situation bothers him so much. He dreams of a vacation where he doesn't have to *bother* with all this. His wife reminds him that if he doesn't *bother* with it, he won't *have* it. "That's okay with me," her husband would say. "It's okay *now*," she would respond, "but wait until you don't have it."

When it comes time for vacation, he just wants to *go*. She wants to go too. She just wants Security to go with them.

Do you recognize yourself or your mate in any of the scenarios above? They typify four areas where the dream of Security commonly surfaces. We could discuss many more, but now it's time to see how *you* relate to the issue of Security. Consider the following questions, and decide whether each one is truer of you or your mate . . .

SECURITY INVENTORY—*Protection*	YOU	MATE
Who always thinks to make sure the kids are warm enough?		
Who is more likely to stay awake during a severe storm?		
Who is more willing to go parasailing or rappelling and take the kids along too?		
Who would rather block the bad channels on the cable TV or not get cable at all?		
Who would rather install Internet monitoring or blocking software?		
Who asks more often where the child is going and with whom?		
Who calls a child's teacher about a mistreatment or confusion in the child's classroom?		
Who always has his or her eye on the younger child?		

SECURITY INVENTORY—*Provision*	YOU	MATE
Who is more eager to save for the future?		
Who is more concerned about a financial plan for retirement or college?		
Who wants to make sure that the details of a trip are taken care of?		
Who makes sure that the family always has what it needs before going somewhere?		
Who saves things for some future use?		
Who is more concerned with providing a way for the child to make friends or get involved?		
Who thinks most about the family's material, social, or spiritual needs?		

Finding the Root

On a scale from one to ten, how important is Security to you? Place an X where you think you belong. Now put an O where you think your mate belongs.

1 ←——————————————————————————————→ 10

Are there recurring arguments in your marriage that you think might be driven by the desire for Security? What are they about?

Do you think there is something from your past that makes your desire for Security especially important to you? Have you ever discussed this with your mate?

Do you think there is something happening in your life right now that could be heightening your desire for Security?

CHAPTER FOUR

Loyalty

Faithfulness and Priority

Tim: Not long ago I got together with some old buddies of
         mine. We went to a friend's beach house for the week-
         end, just the four of us. Just the guys.

Joy: Now there's a recipe for disaster.

Tim: We started talking about how we all met each other for
         the first time. My friend Kent remembered the first
         time we ever met, and I could remember the first time I
         ever saw him. We went around the table, sharing our
         memories, until we came to my friend Mike. He re-
         counted our first meeting, and then everyone turned to
         me and waited—but I just sat there. Finally Mike said,
         "You mean to tell me you can't remember anything
         about the first time we met?" I said, "Oh, please—I get
         enough of that from my wife."

Joy: This is why men should never be allowed to meet in
         groups.

Tim: It was a funny line. Everybody howled! Mike thought it
         was such a great joke that when he got back with me,
         he shared it with Joy. Guess what? Joy didn't think it
         was funny.

Joy: Can you imagine that?

Tim: Joy thought that my little joke was at her expense. I
         told her, "I wasn't laughing at you, honey; I was laugh-
         ing with you."

Joy: And I explained to him that to be laughing with someone, two people have to be laughing.

Tim: I told Joy that it was no big deal—that sometimes
when men get together, they make little jokes about
their wives.

Joy: I said I know. Sometimes wives do the same thing—
and whenever their husbands hear about it later, it
bothers them—and it should.

Tim: I finally began to understand why it mattered to her. It
was more than a joke at Joy's expense; it was an act of
disloyalty. I had said something in private that I would
never have said in her presence. I had painted a picture
of her that was less than flattering—a stereotype of a
nagging, demanding wife that wasn't true of her at all.
Instead of defending Joy, I was demeaning her—and I
was doing it behind her back.

Joy: Every wife wants to know that she can trust her husband, not just in the big things, but in the little things
as well. She wants to know that her husband is loyal—
not only in what he says to her, but in what he says
about her.

Tim: So I learned a good lesson. And I told Mike that I still
couldn't remember the first time we met, but I sure
would remember the last.

Dreaming of Loyalty

Loyalty is the value that asks, "Whose side are you on, anyway?" It's the dream of a mate who is a soul mate—someone
who is unreservedly committed to you and to the relationship.
Consider some comments from our survey that indicate that
the dream of Loyalty is at work . . .

- We repeatedly disagree over outside obligations coming
before me.

60

- *He takes a piece of my heart with every lie.*

- *Why can't he stand up to his father on his family's behalf?*

- *Enjoying time for myself and my hobby doesn't mean I put them first.*

- *I don't understand his quick reaction to others' needs, but not mine.*

- *How can he find so much to talk about with everyone else but not with me?*

- *I want his time to have fun to be with ME!!*

Loyalty has two essential components: *Faithfulness* and *Priority.*

Faithfulness: You Can Count on Me

Faithful is the term we reserve for those precious few we can count on to be truthful, trustworthy, and steadfastly committed to us—and few they are. "Many a man proclaims his own loyalty," Proverbs 20:6 says, "but who can find a trustworthy man?" Faithfulness means being able to count on someone regardless of the issue and regardless of the circumstances. Faithfulness is what we vow first and foremost on our wedding day.

Priority: We Put Each Other First

Priority is something else we vow on our wedding day, though we may not have used that exact word. Priority is what we mean by the phrase "forsaking all others." To "forsake" means "to give up something *formerly held dear.*" The implication is to move someone new into first place in one's life. In the case of marriage, it means to put someone in her *rightful* place. The book of Genesis describes a process for the formation of a marriage relationship: "For this reason a man shall leave his father and his mother, and be joined to his wife; and they shall become one flesh" (Genesis 2:24). For a *Loyal* marriage relationship to be formed, there must be a cutting of ties and a shifting of priorities.

A man lies dying at home on his bed. Suddenly, he awakens! Drifting up the stairs comes the aroma of his favorite of all foods, his wife's special chocolate chip cookies. He drags himself from his bed and down the hallway. At the bottom of the stairway, he pulls himself to his feet and staggers into the kitchen. There on the kitchen table . . . can it be? Yes! *Dozens* of thick, golden-brown cookies! He lurches toward the table and reaches out a trembling arm. . . . Suddenly, a spatula smacks him on the back of the hand.

"Get away from those!" his wife barks. "They're for the funeral!"

We all need to know that the marriage will come before the in-laws, the best friends, the children—even the funeral. We need to know that we are our mate's Priority.

Each of us is born with an instinctive "me first" attitude. But in marriage, each husband and wife has to cultivate a *"we first"* mentality—and each needs to know that his or her partner shares that value. Family therapist Terry Hargrave calls this concept "us-ness." "Instead of pursuing self-fulfillment," he writes, "the partners could dedicate themselves to caring for a third entity: their precious and vulnerable relationship."[1] Hargrave recommends that we think of marriage as a three-party arrangement. There's you, there's me, and there's *us*—and *we* come first.

Amplifying Factors

The most devastating breaches of Loyalty are ones that involve basic marital fidelity. When we speak of a spouse being *unfaithful,* we mean only one thing. Each of us desires our spouse to be faithful in the most basic sense, but the dream of Loyalty goes much deeper. Unseen aspects of Faithfulness and Priority cause conflict in day-to-day married life.

She: *Where have you been?*

He: *At the hardware store. Why?*

She: *All this time? You've been gone for three hours.*

He: *Sometimes I just like to look around.*

She: *What in the world can you look at for three hours?*

He: *I don't know. What do you look at in the mall for three hours?*

She: *Did you stop anywhere else?*

He: *What's with the third degree? I don't have to report to you every time I go out, you know.*

Those who especially value Loyalty are sometimes vulnerable to doubt and thoughts of suspicion. This husband feels like he's being accused of something. *All this time? You've been gone for three hours.*

His wife's desire for Faithfulness and Priority may be amplified by the stories she constantly hears about husbands who are somewhat *less* than faithful. Her best friend's husband asked for a divorce last week, and the woman never saw it coming—she had *no idea.* If that can happen to her best friend, why can't it happen to her?

This wife dreams of Loyalty in a faithless world, and she longs for Priority in a world where women are often *not* a Priority. Even if her husband is a perfectly loyal man, he may still suffer from guilt by association—or at least *suspicion.* It isn't that she doesn't trust *him;* it's just that their marriage is surrounded by so much disloyalty.

He thinks his wife doesn't trust him. He's partly right; this *is* an issue of trust, but it's not entirely about him. Sometimes Loyalty arguments are about the world around you—and it's hard not to take it personally.

He: *Don't forget, Mom is coming over for lunch today.*

She: *Does your mother have to come over for lunch*
every Sunday?

He: *Here we go on my mother again . . .*

She: *It seems like every time we have a spare moment*
you're inviting your mother over.

He: *She lives alone; you know that. She doesn't have*
anyone else.

She: *She has your brother and sister. She's their mother*
*too. Why don't **they** invite her over once in a while?*

He: *Why don't you like my mother? She's always nice*
*to **you**.*

Family researchers tell us that in-laws are one of the most common sources of conflict for married couples. Not necessarily. In-laws are certainly one of the most common *apparent* sources of conflict, but the real dispute is often over something deeper.

The husband and wife in our scenario seem to be having a classic in-law argument. They are indeed—but in-law arguments are often not about moms and dads, but about Loyalty. The wife may actually *love* her mother-in-law, but she resents the *Priority* Mom seems to have in their marriage. The husband assumes that his wife must not *like* his mother. Why else would Mom be unwelcome? As the scenario ends, he is preparing to make the case that his mother is *likable*, and that she *deserves* to be liked—an argument that will go nowhere, because the disagreement was never about Mom's character in the first place.

The conflict isn't about whether Mom should come over, but whether Mom should come *first. It seems like every time we have a spare moment you're inviting your mother over.* She wonders, *Why isn't the same level of initiative and interest being shown in our marriage? First leave, then cleave; sometimes it seems like you never left. Whose side are you on, anyway?*

Dreaming of Shared Priorities

The Loyalty conflict is often about Priority, and it surfaces anytime something else seems to have claimed the attention and desire that you feel *you* rightly deserve, whether that something is a job, a hobby, an Internet site, another person—even your own children.

> *She:*   *I can't believe that in just five years Sarah will go away to college.*
>
> *He:*   *I'm kind of looking forward to it.*
>
> *She:*   *Looking forward to it! Are you kidding?*
>
> *He:*   *I'll miss her, of course. But think of all the things we'll be able to do . . .*
>
> *She:*   *You, maybe, but what about me? The kids have been my whole life!*
>
> *He:*   *Thanks a lot.*

He loves the kids—and he's glad that she loves them too. But when he hears the longing in her voice, he wonders if she feels anything remotely similar for him. It's been a problem for them since their first daughter was born. The wife seemed to love the newborn with an intensity her husband had never experienced himself, and at times he felt twinges of jealousy. When the baby first arrived, he expected his wife's love to expand to *include* the baby; instead, it sometimes seemed as if her love for him had transferred *to* the baby.

It's silly, he tells himself, to be jealous of his own children. He tries to remind himself how lucky he is to be married to a woman who is such a devoted mom—but it doesn't always help. Sometimes he finds himself pulling back from the kids, not because he doesn't love them, but because he resents the Priority they've assumed. *It's always about the kids.* We need to love many people in our lives, but in marriage a person instinctively feels that he deserves a unique place in his mate's heart.

He feels ignored, and he longs to once again become his wife's Priority. But perhaps the reason that his wife has shifted her Priority to the children is that *his* Priorities have wandered as well . . .

> *He:*   *I have to work late again tonight.*
>
> *She:*   *Again? That's the third night this week.*
>
> *He:*   *I can't help it; performance reviews are coming up.*
>
> *She:*   *Last week it was the big audit to get ready for; this week it's performance reviews. It's always something.*
>
> *He:*   *What do you want me to do, quit my job?*
>
> *She:*   *Of course not. I just wish you gave your family the same amount of attention you give your job. Even when you're here, your mind is on some project.*
>
> *He:*   *Why do you think I work as hard as I do? I'm not doing this just for me, you know.*

One of the most difficult balances of life is the tension between work and family. How much time do you spend at the office, and when is it time to come home? Spouses don't always answer these questions the same way, and the resulting argument is often about Loyalty. Ironically, what one partner sees as an act of Faithfulness, the other may see as a lack of Priority.

She understands the demands of his job, and she actually appreciates his dedication. She admires his position and his desire to provide for his family, but she still finds herself pulling back from him, afraid that her attempts to connect with him will be met with a dull "uh-huh" or a blank stare.

Part of the problem is that he never comes home at all—at least, not all of him. She would like him to be home more, but more importantly, when he is home she wants him to be *all there*—not just physically, but in mind and spirit too. When she tries to explain this, he reacts defensively, suggesting that her demands are extreme and unreasonable. *What do you want me to do, quit my job?*

She feels misunderstood and taken for granted. Because he has withdrawn from the kids and no longer seeks to enter their world, she believes she must pull double duty. His lack of initiative in the family lowers her respect for him. She decides that she won't ask for his involvement anymore; she'll simply leave him alone and take care of the family's needs on her own.

If they continue this way, she may never know that he really wants to be a vital part of her world. And sadly, he may never understand that she longs for him to be the hub of the family and have the sense of Priority he desires. It may all be lost in the whirlwind of conflicting desires over Faithfulness and Priority.

> *She:* *Do you think she's pretty?*
>
> *He:* *Who?*
>
> *She:* *You know who.* **Her.**
>
> *He:* *Her? I didn't notice.*
>
> *She:* *You noticed. I can tell when you look at another woman, Tom.*
>
> *He:* *Okay, so I look sometimes. But I don't touch.*
>
> *She:* *Oh,* **that's** *a big comfort.*
>
> *He:* *Look, I'm only human. You expect too much, you know that?*

Husbands sometimes allow their eyes to wander—and wives notice when they do. "I still don't understand why he looks at other women," one wife lamented on our survey. Husbands tend to view an occasional visual tryst as a harmless indiscretion, but wives often see it as something more—as a kind of visual *unfaithfulness*. "You have heard that it was said, 'Do not commit adultery,'" Jesus once said. "But I tell you that anyone who looks at a woman lustfully has already committed adultery with her in his heart" (Matthew 5:27–28 NIV). Loyalty begins in the heart and works outward. True Faithfulness, in other words, is revealed in small things. As Jesus reminded us on another occasion, "Unless you are faithful in small matters, you won't be faithful in large ones" (Luke 16:10 NLT).

"One thing that gets people through difficult spots is fidelity," author Michael Leach writes, "not just fidelity to sexuality, but to the other person's emotions, to compassion, to kindness. Those who value fidelity can get through anything."[2] Those who value Loyalty long to know that their mate is *consistently* faithful, in attitude as well as in action, in public as well as in private, in small matters as well as in large.

> *She:* Boy, this restaurant is expensive.
>
> *He:* Don't worry about it. I'll put it on my expense account.
>
> *She:* How can you do that? This isn't a business meeting.
>
> *He:* I just got back from a business trip, remember? They don't know exactly when I returned, so I just tack it on to the end of the trip. Presto! A free meal.
>
> *She:* Wouldn't they fire you if they found out?
>
> *He:* Who's going to find out? I do this all the time.
>
> *She:* You do? But isn't that . . . dishonest?
>
> *He:* Look, I thought you might like to go to a nice place for a change. We can still go to Burger King, you know.

When Teddy Roosevelt was a young man, he worked as the foreman of a cattle ranch in Colorado. One day one of the ranch hands came to Roosevelt and told him that a stretch of wire had broken down, and several unbranded cattle from the neighboring ranch had wandered through onto their land. "I branded them and mixed them in with our own herd," the man said with a wink.

"Get your gear and get out," Roosevelt said. "You're fired."

The news of the ranch hand's immediate dismissal surprised everyone. After all, hadn't the man acted in his employer's best interests? Isn't that Loyalty? And besides, would the neighboring ranch have even missed a few wandering cattle? Asked about his decision, Roosevelt replied, "A man who will steal *for* me is a man who will steal *from* me."

Roosevelt understood that real Loyalty has no boundaries. A man who is dishonest at work will be dishonest at home. A woman who will talk to you about other people will talk to other people about you. A man who will steal *for* you is a man who will steal *period*.

That's why it's hard to trust the Loyalty of someone who seems to be faithful to nothing or no one else. If you're not loyal to others, can I really be confident that you're faithful to me? Why are you making an exception in my case?

Now it's time to consider how the dream of Loyalty relates to *your* marriage. Consider the following questions and ask whether each of them is true of you always, sometimes, or never.

LOYALTY INVENTORY—*Faithfulness*	ALWAYS	SOMETIMES	NEVER
Do I betray my mate's confidence by the way I talk about him when he's not present?			
Do I joke about my mate in the presence of other people and later find out she is angry about what I said?			
Do I look at the opposite sex in a way that shows interest?			
Does my mate ever express disappointment about the way I notice the opposite sex?			
Could my mate walk in on me in any circumstance without me being uncomfortable?			
Does my mate ever have doubts about my faithfulness?			
Do I confide in my mate above anyone else about my personal issues and concerns?			

LOYALTY INVENTORY—*Priority*	ALWAYS	SOMETIMES	NEVER
Do I find myself having a difficult time saying no to others because their needs seem significant or urgent?			
Does my mate ever voice displeasure with the amount of time I spend with people outside our home?			
Do I sometimes put the needs of my children before the needs of my spouse?			
Does my mate ever voice a feeling of neglect when it comes to his place in our marriage?			
Do I put as much thinking and creativity into my marriage as I do into my work or hobbies?			
Does my mate ever voice regret about being taken for granted?			
Do we have things that we enjoy doing together or talking about other than jobs, children, or the business of running the home?			

Finding the Root

On a scale from one to ten, how important is Loyalty to you? Place an X where you think you belong. Now put an O where you think your mate belongs.

1   10

Are there recurring arguments in your marriage that you think might be driven by the desire for Loyalty? What are they about?

Do you think there is something from your past that makes your desire for Loyalty especially important to you? Have you ever discussed this with your mate?

Do you think there is something happening in your life right now that could be heightening your desire for Loyalty?

CHAPTER five

RESPONSIBILITY

Obligation and Expectation

Joy: Tim and I once took a test called the Keirsey Tempera-
       ment Sorter to help us understand our different personal-
       ities. Each of us had to fill out a seventy-question survey.

Tim: Which was more than my personality wanted to do in
       the first place.

Joy: Our answers were evaluated, and we were told that we
       each had a basic temperament type—a different temper-
       ament type—and that this temperament type predicted
       what we would do and say in different situations. My
       type was called "the most sociable of all types."

Tim: While mine was called "incurable, but at least not con-
       tagious." At least, that's what Joy called it.

Joy: We were each given an article that described our tem-
       perament type in detail. Mine said, "This temperament
       type has a well-developed sense of tradition [and] takes
       the 'rights and wrongs' of the culture seriously." People
       with this temperament type often feel a strong sense of
       obligation and responsibility.

Tim: On the other hand, I was described this way: "Authority
       derived from office, position, or wide acceptance does
       not impress this temperament type. Only statements
       that are logical and coherent carry weight. External

authority per se is irrelevant." People with this tempera-
ment can seem individualistic and even arrogant.

Joy: *You can imagine some of the conversations we've had.*

Tim: *Needless to say, Joy and I have a very different natural sense of Responsibility. I wish I had a dollar for every time we've had a conversation like this . . .*

Joy: *"Are you going to wear those pants?"*

Tim: *"What's wrong with them?"*

Joy: *"They're white. You're not supposed to wear white pants in the winter."*

Tim: *"Who made up that rule?"*

Joy: *"Everybody knows that."*

Tim: *"I don't know that."*

Joy: *"This from a man who wears tennis shoes to church."*

Tim: *(A long pause) "And your point would be?"*

Joy: *"Look, I don't make up these rules. You're just not supposed to wear white in the winter, that's all."*

Tim: *"So someone I never met makes up a rule that makes no sense, and I'm supposed to follow it?"*

Joy: *"Why don't you wear your underwear outside your pants while you're at it?"*

Tim: *And that's about as far as the conversation gets. The problem is, Joy often feels a sense of Responsibility where I feel none. And that, as this chapter describes, often leads to conflict.*

Joy: *Where did you get that shirt?*

Should, Ought, and Must

The *Responsibility* conflict begins with the word *ought*—we *ought* to do this, we *ought* to take care of that. In marriage, one partner often has a greater sense of duty to follow the dictates of laws, customs, fashions, and the expectations of others. These are the rules—we *ought* to consider them. Here are some comments from our survey that suggest the dream of Responsibility . . .

- *I care about how people see me and what they think about us.*
- *I wish she would lighten up and not major on the minors.*
- *Why is she so fussy about traffic laws?*
- *We repeatedly disagree over child rearing. What are the rules?*
- *We disagree about legalism vs. Christianity.*
- *He doesn't see the need to maintain and improve our home and allows it to go downhill.*
- *I don't understand her "black-and-white" approach to life.*
- *We disagree about getting bills paid on time.*

While laws are carefully defined, customs, fashions, and the expectations of others are more ambiguous, and that's what leads to the Responsibility conflict. In marriage, most disagreements don't arise from what's said, but from what's left unsaid—from what's *assumed*—and two different people can have very different assumptions about what *ought* to be done. There are two components of the value of Responsibility: *Obligation* and *Expectation*.

Obligation: What One Owes

Obligation is an internal sense of what is *owed*. Every culture has thousands of unwritten customs and mores that everyone has to learn in order to fit in: It's not polite to stare, the fork goes on the left, never shout in church, and always use a handkerchief (not your sleeve). These are all things we're told we *ought* to do, but each of us has a different sense of just how important it really is to comply. After all, exactly whom are we obeying, and why? Where do these rules and regulations come from? Why were they created? Are they still relevant? Are they reasonable and practical? No one knows the answers, but still that inner feeling of *oughtness* persists. That's what we call Obligation.

Expectation: What Others Require

Whereas Obligation is your sense of how important it is to comply, *Expectation* is your idea of what other people require of you. What do the neighbors expect of me? What do they think I should do? What is appropriate behavior, and when am I "out of line"? When am I in style, and when am I embarrassing myself—or my spouse? Expectation asks the question, "What will people think?"

Different People, Different Rules

To be fair, *all* of us are governed by some internal sense of Obligation and Expectation. No law prevents a man from wearing his underwear outside his pants—but with the exception of a few rock stars, no one does. There is a word for someone who rejects *all* of the Obligations and Expectations of a society: *sociopath*. We all operate within *some* unspoken guidelines of appropriateness and civility; we just don't always agree on what those guidelines are or how important it is that we obey them. This difference in internal value systems is what creates the Responsibility conflict.

> She: *Why are you eating your chicken with your fingers?*
>
> He: *Because it's barbecued chicken. You always eat barbecued chicken with your fingers.*
>
> She: *Not in a restaurant you don't.*
>
> He: *What difference does it make?*
>
> She: *It looks sloppy, for one thing.*

76

He: *It doesn't seem sloppy to me; it seems practical.*

She: *Plus, it makes you look immature.*

He: *Look at that guy over there. See? He's using his fingers.*

She: *He's eating ribs, not chicken.*

He: *What's the difference?*

She: *See that man over there? He's using a knife and fork.*

Responsibility conflicts can begin over the simplest rules —two different *understandings* of the rules. As he sees it, *you always eat barbecued chicken with your fingers.* But to her, there's a proviso in this case: *unless you're in a restaurant.*

They begin to compare rulebooks: Barbecued chicken is in, baked chicken is out; ribs are in, chicken is out. They obviously disagree, so he asks if the rule is really important. The answer is obvious: To him it's not important at all, but to her it is. That's because she has the greater sense of Responsibility.

Now they begin to do two things that rarely work in a Responsibility conflict. First, she tries to convince him of the *reasonableness* of the rule: Eating chicken with your fingers makes you look both sloppy and immature. Not to him—to him it's a matter of simple convenience. So much for being reasonable.

Next, he appeals to the example of others. *That* guy doesn't recognize the rule, so why should I? She in turn searches for her own testimonials. *He's using a knife and fork.*

They may spend the next hour scouring the restaurant for supporters of their own perspective. Dinner may be over before they realize that they were never really arguing about chicken at all. They were arguing about Responsibility.

She: *Why didn't you cut the grass this weekend?*

He: *I didn't have time. I was playing golf, remember?*

She: *Well, you'd better cut it after work today.*

He: It can wait till next Saturday.

She: You're going to leave it like that for a **week**? What will the neighbors think?

He: Who cares what the neighbors think?

She: I care, and so should you.

He: What about the Johnsons next door? They've had that rusty old swing set in their backyard for years. It's an eyesore, but I don't complain about it.

She: I agree, but we can't tell them that.

He: If we can put up with their swing set, then they can put up with our grass.

She: You just don't care about anybody but yourself.

They both know the grass needs to be cut, but they differ as to why. To him, it needs to be cut for purely practical reasons, and so it can wait until another weekend. But to her, the grass needs to be cut for a much more urgent reason: The neighbors *expect* it to be cut.

At least *she* thinks they do. The neighbors have never said so, of course, nor are there any neighborhood covenants or by-laws about the acceptable length of Kentucky Bluegrass. If there were, there would be no disagreement. The Responsibility conflict is about what *isn't* said.

He suggests that their neighbors have also failed to keep some of *their* obligations. *What about the Johnsons next door?* If the neighbors don't follow the rules, why should they? The argument doesn't satisfy her. After all, someone else's failure to act responsibly is no excuse for their *own* disobedience.

They finally arrive at a stalemate with a misunderstanding of the other person's dream. *She* thinks he's just plain selfish, while *he* thinks she cares too much about what other people think. This is how the Responsibility conflict usually ends.

He: *Have you looked at the van lately? It's an unbeliev-
     able mess!*

She: **You** *try driving four kids around all day.*

He: *Why don't you clean it up?*

She: *Why? So the kids can just trash it again?*

He: *What are you saying—you're just going to leave it
     like that forever?*

She: *I'm saying I just haven't gotten around to it.*

He: *Well, you need to get around to it.*

She: *What's the big deal?*

He: *A car should never be allowed to get in that condition.*

This husband and wife would both like to have a clean car,
but for different reasons, and so they come to the argument
with a different sense of priority. For her, cleaning the van is a
low priority. It would be *nice,* but all of the other demands of
raising and transporting four kids come first. She'll clean the
car whenever she gets around to it.

But for him, cleaning the van is a much higher priority, because his desire is fueled by his sense of Responsibility. *A car
should never be allowed to get in that condition.* Why? Who
says so? If you pressed him, he would have a very difficult time
answering those questions—at least to her satisfaction. Maybe
he would be embarrassed if his friends saw the car. Not her; she
thinks her friends should understand. Maybe his own mother
always kept the family station wagon spotless, or maybe his father always complained that she didn't. Whatever the reason,
he now has an inner sense of certainty that a car *ought* to be
kept clean. He has a dream.

And to whom is this Obligation owed? To General Motors?
To the neighbors, who never see the inside of their van? Again,
he would have a difficult time answering. This is a debt owed
to the car, and to their family, and to the universe itself. This is
not about someone else's requirement; this is an internal sense

of Obligation. We *ought* to clean the car because . . . we just *ought* to.

> He: *You need to slow down here. See the sign? Thirty-five miles per hour.*
>
> She: *There's no way this should be a thirty-five zone. Fifty maybe, but not thirty-five.*
>
> He: *They must have had a good reason for making it thirty-five.*
>
> She: *What reason? There isn't a school within ten miles. It's a residential area, but there are no driveways that connect with this street.*
>
> He: *I don't know the reason. All I know is the sign says thirty-five.*
>
> She: *Well, I'm not going to spend the whole day on this street just because somebody put up a sign.*
>
> He: *You can't obey only the laws that make sense to you. What would happen if everybody did that?*
>
> She: *Maybe we wouldn't have so many traffic jams.*

He wants to "obey earthly authorities" because it's the right thing to do. *All I know is the sign says thirty-five.* She wants to drive a little faster because it's the practical thing to do. *I'm not going to spend the whole day on this street just because somebody put up a sign.* In Responsibility conflicts that's often the standoff: *principles vs. pragmatism.* Because he values Responsibility, he always seeks to act out of principle. His first question—sometimes his *only* question—is always, "What is the right thing to do?" After all, what else really matters?

She, on the other hand, always asks, "What is the *best* thing to do?" She doesn't mean best in *principle*—she means the easiest, most sensible, and most convenient. It isn't that she wants to deliberately disobey; it's just that she values something more than obedience—in this case, her time.

She sees her husband as unnecessarily bound by petty restrictions. He sees his wife as stubborn and rebellious. They both agree that "35 MPH" is a rule. To her it's an unreasonable rule that can be disregarded. To him it's still a rule, and it *ought* to be obeyed.

Responsibility to Others

She: *The Andersons are moving this Saturday.*

He: *Oh?*

She: *They're moving themselves, you know. We should offer to help.*

He: *Did they ask for our help?*

She: *You don't wait for people to ask. You offer to help.*

He: *The Andersons have lots of other neighbors who can help them move. Why are we always the ones who have to help out?*

She: *Look, we have to at least drop by and see if they need anything.*

He: *Why do we have to?*

She: *Because that's what neighbors are supposed to do, especially if they're Christians. What will they think if we don't even stop by?*

He: *They'll think we have things to do on a Saturday too.*

This is a true Responsibility conflict, one that involves both Obligation and Expectation. The neighbors are moving—how will they respond? Obligation speaks first. *We should offer to help.* To her, there is a principle involved here: When a neighbor is in need, you *ought* to pitch in. It isn't a matter of convenience; it's simply the right thing to do.

But to him there are practical concerns here. This is a Saturday, after all, and there's a price for helping the Andersons. A day spent loading a truck is a day not fixing their own home or playing with the kids. How important is this? Is their assistance really necessary? *Did they ask for our help?*

To her, this question touches on a second Obligation. *You don't wait for people to ask. You offer to help.* Her unwritten rule is that you ought to help out, and you don't wait to be asked. Perhaps her parents taught her this value, or perhaps she came by it on her own; either way, it's a firm conviction for her now—but not for him. His pragmatic response is that lots of people are available to help the Andersons. *Why are we always the ones who have to help out?*

Obligation is getting nowhere, so now Expectation joins the conversation. If the principle of neighbors-helping-neighbors means nothing to him, he should at least think about what the Andersons will expect. *What will they think if we don't even stop by?* But even the power of Expectation isn't enough to persuade him.

She thinks he's selfish and uncaring, and he thinks she doesn't have to come to the rescue of everyone in need. After she helps load the truck on Saturday, they may continue their discussion about Responsibility.

She: *I've been thinking about your mom. After her last fall, I'm not sure she should live by herself anymore.*

He: *What do you think we should do?*

She: *She should come to live with us, of course.*

He: *With us? You've got to be kidding!*

She: *She's family. You take care of family. You can't just put her in some lonely nursing home.*

He: *My mom would take a lot of care. Do you have any idea how hard that would be on our family?*

She: *John, you take care of family. We don't have a choice.*

Decisions about caring for aging parents are extremely difficult—but for her, there's no decision to make. *She should come to live with us, of course.* To her husband it's a serious dilemma, and he begins to remind her of the potential costs and difficulties of such a decision. *My mom would take a lot of care. Do you have any idea how hard that would be on our family?*

It's not that she's unaware of the potential costs. She isn't naive, and she knows that she may have to pay a great personal price for this decision. It's just that, to her, all potential costs and liabilities are overruled by a single, overpowering principle: *You take care of family.*

The problem is, she has no way to communicate the power of that principle to her husband. She may try to explain it, or justify it, or passionately defend it, but if he doesn't *share* it, he will not feel its *power.*

When her husband questions her decision, she simply repeats the principle. *John, you take care of family.* He cannot understand how she can make such a quick decision about a matter with so many far-reaching implications. To her, it all boils down to a single question: Will we be Responsible?

Do these situations sound familiar? Why not consider the following questions to see how the issue of Responsibility relates to *your* marriage . . .

RESPONSIBILITY INVENTORY—*Obligation*	YOU	MATE
Who pays more attention to social or political issues?		
Who is more conscientious about when the bills are due and paid?		
Who cares more about basic etiquette when it comes to manners and fashion?		
Who is quicker to think that you should help someone in need, whether a neighbor, a friend, or a relief organization around the world?		
Who is more likely to suggest that you volunteer for something at church because it's the right thing to do?		
Who feels more obligated to have someone over because you were previously invited to their home?		
Who in your marriage is the one who writes the thank-you notes?		

RESPONSIBILITY INVENTORY—*Expectation*	YOU	MATE
Who attends the office party even if it's the last place you'd like to be?		
Who feels more of an obligation to keep a commitment even though it becomes inconvenient?		
Who calls if he or she is going to be late or not able to come?		
Who feels more responsible to give money when asked to make a donation?		
Who will return messages and e-mail to people even if it's inconvenient?		
Who feels more strongly that your word is your bond?		
Who considers the opinions of others rather than pleasing only himself?		

Finding the Root

On a scale from one to ten, how important is Responsibility to you? Place an X where you think you belong. Now put an O where you think your mate belongs.

1   10

Are there recurring arguments in your marriage that you think might be driven by the desire for Responsibility? What are they about?

Do you think there is something from your past that makes your desire for Responsibility especially important to you? Have you ever discussed this with your mate?

Do you think there is something happening in your life right now that could be heightening your desire for Responsibility?

CARING

Awareness and Initiative

Joy: *When Tim and I were first married, I thought it would be nice if he would call me from the office from time to time.*

Tim: *One day Joy asked me, "If you think of me during the day, why don't you call me?"*

Joy: *And he said, "Because I don't think of you."*

Tim: *That was a big win.*

Joy: *I thought as a newlywed I might have made a little more of an impression. I knew that Tim had a tendency to get lost in his work, but I guess I thought I might accidentally pop into his thoughts once in a while.*

Tim: *I did start calling you after that, remember?*

Joy: *That was very nice. Then one day I realized that you had put a Post-It on your phone that said, "Call Joy." That's when I realized that you hadn't spontaneously started to think about me; you were just obeying a sign—like "Pay electric bill."*

Tim: *Isn't the important thing that I called?*

Joy: *I didn't need more phone calls. I just wanted to know that you cared.*

Tim: *In our marriage, Joy and I have had a lot of discussions about Caring. To put it bluntly, I will never care as much as Joy does about anything. Joy is a very Caring person. She cares about the kids, their friends, the teachers, the neighbors, even people on the other side of the planet. If Joy knows you, she cares about you.*

Joy: *Sometimes I wish I could care less, because it takes a lot of energy to care about everything. But I'm not sure how to turn it off. I do wish that I could mind-meld some of my Caring to Tim so I don't have to do it all myself.*

Tim: *I do care.*

Joy: *Yes, you do—but sometimes I have to ask you to.*

Tim: *By the way, how did you know about the Post-It on my phone?*

Joy: *I listen to your voice. I care.*

Caring for Each Other

The word *Caring* literally means "feeling and exhibiting concern and empathy for others." The second chapter of Job tells us that when Job's three friends heard of his calamity, they "made an appointment together to come to sympathize with him and comfort him." Their first priority was to empathize, to feel what their friend felt—to Care. That's exactly what they did: "They sat down on the ground with him for seven days and seven nights with no one speaking a word to him, for they saw that his pain was very great" (Job 2:11b, 13). It's a great source of encouragement when people are willing to Care—and a common source of conflict when they're not.

Here are some comments from our survey that reveal underlying Caring disputes . . .

- *I still don't understand why I can do nothing and be in trouble the next time we get together.*

- *I need to be told more of the time that he loves me.*

- *I wish she wouldn't say "nothing" when I ask if something is bothering her.*

- *If I think something is important and he knows it, why doesn't he care enough to at least think about it?*

- *I don't want to be so "responsible" for the marriage and family. I want help.*

- *I don't understand what she needs from me to feel loved and cared for. I need concrete examples—like, "Here's what you're already doing; now this is what I want."*

- *I need him to "show" me rather than "tell" me that he loves me. I want cards, small gifts, etc., rather than the once- or twice-a-year large gifts.*

- *I don't understand why she tells others how much she loves me but has a hard time telling me.*

There are two components of Caring, and one flows from the other like a river from a stream. The stream is *Awareness,* and the river it produces is *Initiative.*

Awareness: Attentiveness to Your Mate

Awareness is mental and emotional alertness, an attitude of attentiveness to your mate's feelings and concerns. "Know well the condition of your flocks," Proverbs 27:23 warns us, and flock-watching is the primary activity of a Caring mate. We want our partners to notice little things, like when we're discouraged, or frustrated, or when we have both legs amputated below the knee—and we don't want to have to tell them. Flock-watching is exhausting when you have to do it alone, especially when those lambs begin to wander. We want our mate to Care enough to know how the sheep—and the shepherd— are doing.

Initiative: The Willingness to Engage

Initiative is what flows naturally from Awareness—at least it should. Initiative is the willingness to *engage* your mate about the problem. It's encouraging to know that your mate is at least conscious of your concern, but it means a lot more when he's willing to *do* something about it. Awareness without Initiative is like faith without works—it is "dead, being by itself." In fact, Awareness without Initiative is sometimes worse than no Awareness at all. It's little comfort to know that your mate is aware of your burden but unwilling to lift a finger to help. In the reassuring words of Homer Simpson, "Just because I don't care, that doesn't mean I don't understand."

Caring Women

Most of the Seven Conflicts are not gender-specific. Loyalty and Responsibility issues, for example, belong to men and women alike. Caring is different; concerns about a lack of Caring are voiced far more often by women than men. As Susan Page writes, "Women's primary complaint about men is that they don't participate in the relationship enough. This objection takes many forms, but they boil down to the same root complaint: men are spaced out, preoccupied, not available."[1]

Women complain that their husbands are not aware and that they do not initiate—and this is the beginning of the Caring conflict.

She: I hate to have to ask this, but how do I look?

He: You look great.

She: Thanks a lot.

He: I said you look great. What's wrong with that?

She: What's wrong is that I have to ask you. Why don't you notice these things on your own? You don't notice because you don't care.

He: I do care. And I do notice how you look—I just forget to say it.

She: Really. So how do you like my hair?

He: Your hair?

She: I got it cut a week ago.
He: Oh . . . it looks great.

"How do I look?" a woman asks her husband. "You look great," he replies. As far as he knows, everything is fine. He responded to her simple question with a positive, enthusiastic response. He's unaware that a Caring conflict is already under way.

He missed the first part of her message: *I hate to have to ask this.* And she does—she hates the feeling that she has to *ask* for praise. It makes her feel small and selfish to have to say, "I'm dressed up today—did you notice?" She wonders why she always has to point out the obvious to him. *So how do you like my hair? I got it cut a week ago.* She offers a rationale for his lack of Awareness. *You don't notice because you don't care.* "I do care," he replies. He just doesn't notice. He can't be expected to notice every picky little thing that changes from day to day.

But his wife knows that he *does* notice picky little things. He notices home runs, new cars, and clever commercials on TV. He notices the things that he cares about—he just doesn't notice *her.*

The first step in Caring is simple Awareness. There will be no compliments or words of praise until he first begins to *notice.* As a friend of ours puts it, "If you were more *thinkful,* you might be more *thoughtful.*"

She: I want to talk about the kids.
He: What is it now?
She: It's Jimmy. He's just so shy.
He: He'll grow out of it.
She: How do you know?
He: I did.
She: But he's not you.
He: I wouldn't worry about it.
*She: You wouldn't worry about **anything.***

In marriage, one partner often carries the *emotional* burden of the family much more than the other. Some of us approach life in a cognitive way; we take a logical, factual, arms-length approach to problems and trials. We think first and feel later—if we feel at all. We're able to compartmentalize problems and put them out of mind when we need to.

Others don't possess this facility. They are more emotionally oriented, and they feel the full emotional weight of every problem or concern. They long to release their burden, but the only way they can do so is by sharing it with someone else—someone who might not be thrilled at the prospect.

She's concerned about Jimmy. *He's just so shy.* She not only sees his problem; she *feels* it. She knows the awkwardness and isolation that shyness brings, and she worries that Jimmy's shyness is a possible indicator of an even larger problem down the road.

But her husband isn't concerned at all. *He'll grow out of it,* he reassures his wife, but his words offer little comfort. His words reveal less about Jimmy than they do about his own approach to problems in general: *I wouldn't worry about it.* It's true, and his wife knows it. *You wouldn't worry about anything.* Why does she have to be the only one who cares?

He thinks that shyness is a minor problem that will pass away with time, and he might be right. But he thinks there's no reason for concern, and that's where he has made his mistake. He needs to be concerned because his *wife* is concerned. Their discussion began about Jimmy, but in a few minutes they'll be arguing about Caring.

She: *Can I talk to you about something?*

He: *Sure.*

She: *A month ago we talked about how the kids need to learn more about the Bible.*

He: *Right. I remember.*

She: *That's not really important to you, is it?*

He: *What do you mean? Of course that's important to me.*

She: *But you haven't done anything about it. I waited a month to mention it again.*

He: *Well, things have been really busy. I've had a lot on my mind. But that doesn't mean I don't care about it.*

She: *How can you say you **care** about it if you won't **do** anything about it? You do the things you care about.*

He: *That's not true. I care about lots of things that I just can't get around to.*

A month ago she talked with her husband about a concern for the kids. *Right*, he replies, *I remember.* He hasn't forgotten, and he hasn't changed his mind—he just hasn't made any changes.

For an entire month she has waited for him to take the Initiative, but nothing has happened. She concludes that he must not care, because true Caring leads to action. *How can you say you **care** about it if you won't **do** anything about it?*

But he believes that Caring simply involves *concern. Of course that's important to me.* He's concerned about the problem, and that means he cares. He's right—Caring *does* involve concern, but true Caring doesn't stop there. Concern is just a form of Awareness, and Awareness has to be followed by Initiative.

As the disagreement progresses, he will argue that he *does* care because he's *concerned,* and she will argue that he *doesn't* care because he doesn't *act.* He thinks he cares because he is aware of the problem; to her, Awareness alone is not enough.

Caring Enough to Engage

Initiative doesn't always require major projects or Herculean efforts. Sometimes all it requires is a simple willingness to *engage* . . .

She: *(Lets out a long sigh)*
He: *(Hears, but ignores her, and continues to read his paper)*
She: *Boy . . .*
He: *You okay?*
She: *I'm fine.*
He: *(Returns to his paper)*
She: *(Another sigh)*
He: *You sure you're okay?*
She: *I guess so . . .*
He: *(Returns to his paper with increased intensity)*

This is the beginning of one of the most common Caring arguments. In this stage, three things have become obvious to both of them: (1) Something is bothering her, (2) He is aware of it to some extent, and (3) He doesn't care enough to pursue it any further. He is about to learn the two mathematical principles that underlie most Caring conflicts: *Awareness + Initiative = Caring,* and *Awareness – Initiative = Conflict.*

Later in the evening, the Caring conflict moves to a more advanced stage . . .

He: *You seem angry. Is something wrong?*
She: *Are you just noticing this now?*
He: *I asked you this afternoon how you were doing. You said you were fine.*

She: I didn't want to interfere with your precious newspaper. How clueless can you get?

He: If something was bothering you, why didn't you
say so?

She: A lot you care.

He: If I didn't care, why would I have asked?

That afternoon, something *was* bothering her—but now
it's something quite different. Her discouragement rapidly
evolved into a Caring conflict when her husband failed to care
enough to engage her about her burden. He doesn't understand that Caring is all about *Initiative*. He thinks he deserves
credit just for asking. But she didn't want him to simply ask;
she wanted him to *care*.

But he did ask, and she said she was fine. *If something was
bothering you, why didn't you say so?* She didn't say so because he didn't really ask. To someone who appreciates Caring,
"You okay?" is not a question at all—it's a throwaway line,
like "What's up?" or "How's it going?" His question was just a
cliché that indicated no real concern or eagerness to understand, and as Paul Tournier reminds us, "People confide their
problems to us in accordance with our readiness to listen."

The husband in our scenario was Aware, but he did not
Initiate—and so, in the eyes of his wife, he didn't really care.

She: What's the matter?

He: I was playing golf with some new guys today. You
should have seen their equipment—top-dollar stuff.
And I've got these lousy, tarnished old golf clubs . . .

She: Were you off your game?

He: It's not that. I just kept looking at their equipment,
and then back at mine. . . . You know, sometimes I feel
like I'm ten years behind where I should be at my age.

She: Try some chrome polish. That should shine them up.

Communication is much more than the simple exchange of information. It also serves to reveal fears, express desires, and disclose secret longings. We communicate not only through our words, but through the tone of our voice, the tightness of our jaw, and the tremor in our hand. Real communication sometimes takes place through "groanings too deep for words," and a Caring listener searches for the meaning *underneath* the message.

Something is bothering him. He isn't sure how to put it into words, so he begins with a comment about golf. *I've got these lousy, tarnished old golf clubs.* She assumes that this is an exchange of information, so she responds in kind. *Were you off your game?* It soon becomes clear that he is not concerned about golf clubs at all—clear, that is, to everyone but her.

Caring is the willingness to work through the complexity and confusion of someone else's emotions, something that the unCaring find bothersome and draining. As a friend of ours expresses it, "I want a man who is strong enough to handle me when I'm a mess, and not just walk away when he doesn't know what to do."

It's easier to recommend a little chrome polish than to wade through the messiness of a midlife crisis. Maybe she was unaware, or maybe she failed to Initiate. In either case, from her husband's perspective she didn't Care.

She: *I picked up your dry cleaning today.*

He: *Good.*

She: *And I took the Chevy in for an oil change. You said that needed to be done.*

He: *It did.*

She: *I picked up **your** dry cleaning and I took **your** car in so **you** wouldn't have to take care of it yourself.*

He: *What do you want, a medal?*

She: A simple "thank you" would be nice, instead of just grunting "good." You act like I owe you something. I do these things for you, you know.

He: Did you ever stop to think how many things I do for you? I cut the grass and pay the bills and fix everything that breaks. Am I supposed to say "thank you" every time you do something around here?

She: It wouldn't kill you once in a while.

The most basic form of Initiative is simply expressing *appreciation*. In marriage, we perform a hundred daily acts of service for each other, and we usually do it without thought of recognition or reward. But from time to time we begin to feel taken for granted: *Does he understand that I'm doing this for him?*

The wife in our scenario points out a simple chore she performed on her husband's behalf. *I picked up your dry cleaning today.* She is saying, "I did a chore *for you,*" but all he hears is, "I did a chore," and so his response is simply, "Good." But he missed the point of her message entirely. She was saying, "Are you *aware* that I did something for you today?"

She offers another example of her service, and once again he misses the underlying message. Finally, she's forced to come right out and make her point directly. *I picked up **your** dry cleaning and I took **your** car in so **you** wouldn't have to take care of it yourself.* Because he's joining the conversation late, he views her blunt request for recognition as arrogant and self-centered. *What do you want, a medal?*

In a healthy marriage, both husband and wife are motivated by a desire to please each other, and we want our mate to understand this motivation. *I do these things for you, you know.* We don't want a medal; we just want our efforts to be recognized. We want to be *appreciated.*

Over the course of years, the daily things we do for each other become so commonplace that we're no longer *aware* of them. At other times we *are* aware, but we take these acts of service for granted. We fail to express appreciation, and the result is often a Caring conflict. "You see all the things I do around here. Don't you *Care?*"

What role does Caring play in your marriage? Who puts the greater value on Awareness and Initiative? The following questions will help you decide . . .

CARING INVENTORY—*Awareness*	YOU	MATE
Who pays more attention to how a person "sounds" and the "body language" when someone else is speaking?		
Who asks, "What's wrong?" and genuinely wants the truth?		
Who is more aware of how the kids are doing emotionally?		
Who is the one that other people come to when they are having a problem?		
Who will not want to discuss his hurts unless he feels that he is being genuinely cared about?		
Who seems to care deeply about others, even strangers that he hears about on the news?		

CARING INVENTORY—*Initiative*	YOU	MATE
Who will try to meet a need before even being asked to help?		
Who takes the initiative in wanting to talk about the problems in your marriage?		
Who is usually the first one to suggest that something should be done about a problem or an injustice?		
Who will take the initiative to go to the school and talk to a teacher about a situation?		
Who takes more of the initiative in the area of intimacy and romance?		
Who needs appreciation because he often puts his own needs second?		
Who verbalizes more interest in your children's spiritual growth?		
Who is more willing to sacrifice time and money to help someone else?		

Finding the Root

On a scale from one to ten, how important is Caring to you? Place an X where you think you belong. Now put an O where you think your mate belongs.

1   10

Are there recurring arguments in your marriage that you think might be driven by the desire for Caring? What are they about?

Do you think there is something from your past that makes your desire for Caring especially important to you? Have you ever discussed this with your mate?

Do you think there is something from your past that makes Caring especially *difficult* for you? Have you ever discussed this with your mate?

Do you think there is something happening in your life right now that could be heightening your desire for Caring?

ORDER

Structure and Control

Tim: *As you may have figured out by now, Joy and I take a different approach to a lot of things—including vacations.*

Joy: *Tim's idea of a vacation is to "head out on the highway, looking for adventure." He just wants to get in the car and go. To me, vacations don't work that way, especially when you have three kids.*

Tim: *Joy wants to plan things out in advance to make sure everything is taken care of and to make sure we get the most out of the vacation.*

Joy: *I want to make the most of the time because we're never sure when a time like this will come again.*

Tim: *For me, the very thing that makes free time free is the lack of Order. What I enjoy most is not knowing what the day will bring. I live under a schedule all week—who wants to do it again on vacation? The lack of planning is what makes the time enjoyable.*

Joy: *Which is great, but with four other people involved, everyone can't just do things their own way.*

Tim: *This difference in our approach to Order even extends to how we spend our spare time. When the kids were young I would say to Joy, "We've got a couple of hours before dinner. Why don't you get out of the house for a while?"*

Joy: And I would say, "Get out? Get out where?"

Tim: "Anywhere. Just go out and have fun."

Joy: "This kind of time is so rare—with no planning, I can't make the most of the time. If I just go, it won't be fun."

Tim: "Okay then, I'll be at Home Depot."

      I was offering Joy exactly what would satisfy **me**—a chunk of free, unstructured time. But that was precisely the kind of time she found frustrating. It took a while before we realized that we had different attitudes about Order.

The Order of Our Lives

Some people like their ducks in a row. Others *have* ducks, but they're not exactly sure where they put them. Some prefer things organized, orderly, and predictable. They want things to go according to plan. They like to know where everything is, and they want to know what comes next. But others would rather take life as it comes. They prefer things spontaneous, unexpected, and unpredictable.

Life is comparatively simple for a just-married couple, but it grows increasingly complex as the years go by. With children, school, home maintenance, and a thousand other concerns to balance, Order becomes a critical issue and a source of great frustration—as some of the responses to our survey indicate:

- *I can't keep the house clean like he expects it. He thinks this is my lack of love and respect toward him because it is a priority to him.*

- *My husband has trouble with organization and leaves his things in piles in the dining room, office, etc.*

- *Why can't he be punctual? We are often late to things, and it causes stress to me because I want to be on time.*

- *We have differing standards of housekeeping. He wants the house "company clean" all the time, but we have six children.*

- *She always forgets to update the checkbook.*

- *He always says, "I'm going to have to get it back out tomorrow; why put it away tonight?"*

- *Why does she worry so much about things out of her control?*

Order conflicts involve fundamental differences in attitude. The argument may begin about finances, or personal records, or the way you spend your time, but it ultimately reduces to one of two underlying issues: the desire for *Structure* or the desire for *Control*.

Structure: A Plan for Everything

Structure is the dream of having a place for everything and everything in its place, but it's much more than that. The desire for Structure can extend not only to household organization, but also to time, work, hobbies, shopping, leisure, and even sex. The underlying conviction is that *anything works better with a plan.* It's more efficient, more thorough, more purposeful, and a better use of resources—and therefore more enjoyable. Enjoyable, that is, if you happen to like Structure. For others, Structure is the very antithesis of enjoyment. How can you enjoy something that feels rigid, contrived, and predictable?

In chapter 3 we said that Security often requires you to limit your freedom in some way. Structure requires even more. Structure requires constant forethought, planning, and discipline. That's a high price to pay, but the price is well worth it to some, because Structure makes possible the second element of Order: *Control.*

Control: Staying in Charge

Control is the desire to somehow keep a firm grip on the steering wheel of life. We live in a world of unseen danger, financial setback, unexpected illness, and even random acts of terrorism. It's an uncertain world, and if you're not careful the car can get away from you. How can you increase your chances of success and minimize your risk of setback or disaster? By maintaining Control. And what better way to maintain Control than through forethought, planning, and discipline? If things are in Order, they're under Control—at least the odds seem more in your favor. As Louis Pasteur once put it, "Chance always favors the prepared mind."

Conflicts Over Order

Let's consider some common disagreements that can occur when ducks get out of line . . .

He: *I can't find your Visa receipts—again.*

She: *They're right over there.*

He: *Where?*

She: *On my desk. Look under that newspaper.*

He: *Your desk is a disaster! You need to keep this clean. You're supposed to put your Visa receipts in this box, remember?*

She: *Aren't they under the newspaper? See, here they are.*

He: *That's not the point. The point is, you're supposed to put them in the box.*

She: *The point isn't to find the receipts?*

He can't find her Visa receipts, and that not-so-subtle word "again" reminds her that it's not the first time. She organizes like an archaeologist, leaving receipts, papers, and unpaid

106

bills buried in various geological strata throughout the house. "Out of sight, out of mind" is her motto, so she attempts to keep things accessible by laying everything out atop desks, end tables, dressers—atop every flat surface in the house until there *is* no more space, and then she starts over again with more recent items on top.

Strangely, this system works for her. *Where are your Visa receipts? They're on my desk, under that newspaper.* If you need anything, just ask her—but you *will* have to ask her, because no one else can understand her mysterious system. So what? It's all the system she needs, so why do more? After all, *isn't the point to find the receipts?*

Not to him. To him, the point is to establish some kind of Structure. Even if her system works, it still drives him crazy because it's disorganized, haphazard, and undependable. They both want to find the Visa receipts, but he wants something more. He wants Order.

He: *What time is everyone supposed to get here?*

She: *I put "7:30 SHARP" on the invitations. You greet people at the door, and I'll get started on the refreshments.*

He: *Whatever.*

She: *We'll let them mingle until eight o'clock. Then we'll move people into the family room and start the game.*

He: *What if people don't feel like playing a game?*

She: *They need to, because that's all I've got scheduled until 9:30.*

He: *For Pete's sake, can't we just relax and have fun?*

There's nothing wrong with relaxing and having fun, but the woman in our scenario has difficulty doing both at the same time. Without a schedule there would be no Structure.

She's in charge of the party, and a schedule is the best way to ensure that people have fun—or so she thinks. *They need to play a game, because that's all I've got scheduled until 9:30.* For those who value Structure, the best way to guarantee a good time is to schedule it in. For others, a party doesn't really get started until it gets out of Control.

Parties are common sources of Order conflicts, because one partner often bears more of the burden for planning and preparing the details of the event. Every party requires *some* Structure. You can't just throw open the doors and see who wanders in, and you'd rather not have strangers searching through your fridge for something to eat. There are invitations to send out, an apartment to clean, and hors d'oeuvres to prepare. If you're not the one who shoulders these responsibilities, it's easy to just sit back and "let the evening happen." But when you're the one in charge, it's happening to *you.*

We sometimes argue about our approach to leisure activities because time off together is so rare. We have to make the most of this opportunity; who knows when we'll get another chance? Both partners agree on this—but they *disagree* about exactly how to do it. For her, the best way to maximize the moment is through Structure and Control. But he lives with Structure and Control all week. For him, the very *absence* of Order is what distinguishes work from leisure.

They think they're arguing about who needs to plan ahead or who needs to relax and let his hair down, but they're really arguing about Order. The question they have to resolve is, "How much Structure does it take to have fun?"

He: *Okay, what's the next item on the list?*
She: *We need a birthday present for your mom.*
He: *Check. Where do we look first?*
She: *I don't know . . . How about that gift shop over there?*
He: *Why that gift shop?*

She: *Why? Because it's right there.*

He: *Let's head to the mall first. When we get there we'll split up and hit the big department stores first. We'll each make a list of possible gift ideas, then we'll meet by the food court in half an hour to compare lists and decide where to go to make the final purchase.*

She: *I hate shopping with you.*

Some people approach shopping the same way they would approach storming the beaches at Normandy—and why not? If you asked them, they would tell you the same elements are important to success in both endeavors: a clear mission, good reconnaissance, a specific timetable. The problem is, some people approach *everything* as if it were an amphibious assault—and for the partner who doesn't favor Structure and Control, this approach is exhausting. *I hate shopping with you.*

She doesn't hate Order itself; she just hates to see it invoked unnecessarily. As we said before, Order requires *effort*—forethought, planning, and discipline. Do we really have to create an agenda just to buy a birthday gift?

For some people who love Order, the answer is yes. This is not just about buying a present; this is about conducting a successful shopping trip—one in which we are organized, aggressive, and thorough. Sure, we can buy a gift anywhere, but we can't find the *best* gift without Order.

The Time and Place for Order

We all know Order is necessary sometimes—but exactly when? When is Order desirable and helpful, and when does it just seem annoying and even compulsive? Sometimes conflicts about Order are also about *timing.*

Some would say that Structure and Control are *always* useful. Others would say, "For crying out loud, we're only *shopping.*"

She: *I'll be back in about three hours. You're sure you'll be okay with little Johnny?*

He: *No problem. Have a good time.*

She: *His favorite books are in a basket by his closet.*

He: *Check.*

She: *You could take him for a walk. It's a nice day.*

He: *Right. Whatever.*

She: *After his walk, he likes to . . .*

He: *Look, I'll take care of it. He's in good hands.*

She: *You're not planning to do any of those things, are you? You're just going to sit there and read the paper the whole time.*

He: *Are you leaving or not?*

Spouses sometimes accuse their partners of being *controlling* —an expression that often means, "You want more Structure than I do." The woman in our scenario offers her husband a series of suggestions for maximizing his time with little Johnny, and she does so for two reasons. First, because that's the approach *she* would take with little Johnny. She's a hands-on mom, and every day she looks for ways to increase her interaction with her son. She expects no more from her husband than what *she* is willing to give.

Second, she knows that Johnny's time alone with his father is in short supply. She sees this as a rare opportunity for both of them, and the best way to maximize the experience is through Structure. *His favorite books are in a basket by his closet. You could take him for a walk . . .*

But her husband feels crowded and resentful. A less-Structured approach is what he was planning—or, more accurately, *not* planning. If Johnny wants to play ball, they'll play ball. If Johnny wants to read a book, they'll read a book. This is play time, and he doesn't need a schedule to play with his own son.

Order conflicts are not always rooted in personality differences. You may desire Order in one situation and resent it in the next. Sometimes we just disagree about when Structure and Control are important.

She: Did you get the new lawn mower put together?
He: It doesn't work. I'm taking it back.
She: What's wrong with it?
He: How should I know? I should have bought a better model. Look at all these extra parts that came with it.
She: Extra parts? Jim, did you read the directions before you put it together?
He: Of course not. Any idiot can put a lawn mower together.

If Order is not your passion, there is no more annoying question than, "Did you read the directions?" *Of course not.* Directions are for fools, meant only for those who lack the insight and intuition to figure out a problem for themselves. Assembling a product should be a spontaneous event—like *all* events—and the only necessary part of the directions is the cover, which shows an image of the finished product to get you headed in a general direction.

People who work in customer service are frequently amazed by the aversion some people have to instruction manuals. They don't really hate instruction manuals—just instructions. They resent the idea of having to lay out all the necessary tools, and clear off an adequate and well-ventilated workspace, and count all the wing nuts and clevis pins before they begin.

But lawn-mower manufacturers should not take this personally. These same people bake cookies without recipes, build gazebos without blueprints, and overhaul engines without consulting the repair manual. Needless to say, not all of these endeavors come out as well as planned—but then, they *weren't* planned. They were done for the sheer enjoyment of working freely without restriction or annoyance.

If you're the one who appreciates Order, it's hard to watch your partner build a gazebo that looks more like the kids' treehouse, knowing all the time that a peek or two at the blueprint would have made all the difference. But just as you may dream of Order, your mate may value freedom and spontaneity with equal passion.

He: Honey, can I make a suggestion?

She: Sure.

He: Every time you put the rubber spatula away, you put it in a different drawer.

She: So? At least I put it away.

He: But I can never find it. Now, suppose we reorganize these drawers according to function. Cooking implements here, mixing implements here, and miscellaneous items here.

She: I don't want to have to memorize a filing system just to clean the kitchen!

He: But it's so simple, and it makes things so much more efficient.

She: I can always find the spatula—look, it's right here.

He: I make one suggestion and you have a cow.

She: I have a suggestion for you. Want to hear it?

A classic marital conflict occurs when a husband retires and suddenly brings his unharnessed creative energies to bear on his wife's household, sometimes resulting in the mysterious and untimely demise of the husband. He spent the last forty years as an accountant, or an engineer, or a systems analyst. He's been in her kitchen thousands of times before, but now, when he really *looks* at it for the first time, he sees dozens of confusing and inefficient systems that could benefit from his knowledge and expertise.

The problem, of course, is that she doesn't *want* his knowledge and expertise. His complaint is that he can't find the rubber spatula. So what? This is *her* kitchen, and she can find the rubber spatula whenever she wants it. This is *his* problem, but he sees it as hers. *Honey, can I make a suggestion?* She finds his suggestion obtrusive and even arrogant. He finds her response shortsighted and unappreciative. *But it's so simple, and it makes things so much more efficient.* But this is not about efficiency; this is about Order—*his* idea of Order.

In marriage, even though we become one flesh, we still have private domains that belong to each of us. It's one thing for you to seek to Structure and Control *your* world, but it's another thing when you're seeking to Order mine. Nothing is easier to organize than someone else's life. We all leave nooks and crannies purposely unstructured, not because we dislike Order, but because no one else's sense of Order seems to suit us. Sometimes the Order conflict is about whose *idea* of Order will rule.

Now it's time to consider the question of Order in relation to *your* relationship. How much do you value Structure and Control in your marriage? Respond to the following questions with always, sometimes, or never.

ORDER INVENTORY—*Structure*	ALWAYS	SOMETIMES	NEVER
Do I prefer to keep a filing system with my papers organized in specific places (versus having a general idea of where they are)?			
Do I put family photos in an album or in chronological order (versus tossing them in a box or drawer)?			
Do I know the kids' schedules and plan ahead for upcoming events (versus grabbing what I need as I go out the door)?			
Do I keep a running "to-do list" (versus doing what I need to do as it unfolds)?			
Do I follow directions, recipes, or sewing patterns (versus "winging it")?			
Do my areas of the house tend to accumulate clutter?			
Do I make a list of what to pack and what needs to be done before a trip (versus dumping the laundry baskets into the sunroof)?			
Do I enjoy watching home improvement shows (versus hyperventilating at the sight of Martha Stewart)?			

ORDER INVENTORY—*Control*	ALWAYS	SOMETIMES	NEVER
Do I enjoy it when people drop by unannounced?			
Am I frustrated when someone interrupts my schedule?			
When I am in charge, am I more comfortable with a detailed plan?			
Would I prefer to be surprised by a special event (versus being in on the planning)?			
Do I have a "hands-on approach" with my kids, knowing where they are and what they're doing most of the time (versus a looser "I'm sure they're okay" approach)?			
Would I rather operate from a budget knowing exactly what I spend (versus knowing I have enough, but not knowing exactly where it's gone)?			
Would I prefer to have some kind of structure on my days off?			

Finding the Root

On a scale from one to ten, how important is Order to you? Place an X where you think you belong. Now put an O where you think your mate belongs.

1   10

Are there recurring arguments in your marriage that you think might be driven by the desire for Order? What are they about?

Do you think there is something from your past that makes your desire for Order especially important to you? Have you ever discussed this with your mate?

Do you think there is something happening in your life right now that could be heightening your desire for Order?

CHAPTER EIGHT

OPENNESS

Sociability and Energy

Joy: *If you haven't guessed it by now, I'm an extrovert. I'm what psychologists refer to as an "Open" personality.*

Tim: *While I, of course, am just the opposite. "Sorry— We're Closed."*

Joy: *Open personalities are often called extroverts. Extroverts like to be around people. We enjoy conversation, and we feel recharged by relationships with others.*

Tim: *Introverts like people, too, but not so many and not all at once. We feel recharged by being alone, and conversation wears us out—especially conversation with strangers.*

Joy: *Tim has a button that says, "Go ahead and talk—I'll just be napping here."*

Tim: *And Joy has a sign on her door that reads, "Extrovert at work—Please interrupt me."*

Joy: *Tim has a clever way of letting his listener know if he's getting tired of the conversation. I learned this after about two days of marriage.*

Tim: *I turn my body away from the other person and I take one step away. Then I sort of rock back and forth a little bit . . .*

Joy: *It's his subtle way of saying, "This plane is going down and I'm bailing out."*

Tim: *It's actually very rude, and I try not to do it—but the temptation is always there. It takes energy to interact with people, and when you're an introvert, energy is always in short supply.*

Joy: *Open personalities are recharged by people, and closed personalities are exhausted by people.*

Tim: *You can imagine the difficulty we've had trying to come to agreement about friendships, parties, and social gatherings of every kind.*

Joy: *We've had to work hard to adjust to each other. There are still a few things we need to improve, though . . .*

Tim: *Excuse me, this is where I bail out.*

Balancing Sociability and Privacy

Openness has to do with your attitude toward people and your need for privacy. Do groups of people invigorate you, or are your batteries drained by social interaction? Do you prefer large social gatherings; small, intimate groups; or no groups at all? Where do you instinctively go when you need to *recharge* —do you seek the company of others, or do you search for some space of your own?

Husbands and wives are sometimes very different when it comes to Openness, as these comments from our survey illustrate . . .

- *My quietness is not a measure of my love for her.*

- *My need for individual time is not a rejection of him.*

- *I have a need for other women's friendships. It's okay to have an occasional cup of coffee without guilt.*

- *I need quiet time and alone time daily—not away from him, just time to be able to reflect and allow God to keep me balanced.*

- *She doesn't understand my lack of enthusiasm and energy at home—I gave everything I had at work.*

- *I don't understand his lack of need for relationships.*

We all desire some amount of intimacy and interaction with others, while at the same time longing for some time to ourselves. In marriage, everyone lives with this tension—but by nature, some of us want far more interaction than others, and that's when Openness conflicts begin. Openness has two chief components: *Sociability* and *Energy.*

Sociability: Desire for People

Sociability is the desire to be with other people, whether a single companion or an entire assembly. Far more than simply being "friendly" or "outgoing," Sociability is an orientation that finds its greatest fulfillment through connection with others. Sociable personalities are traditionally referred to as *extroverts,* while their privacy-seeking counterparts are known as *introverts.* Whereas extroverts are Sociable, introverts are territorial— they seek private places both in the mind and in the world around them. Extroverts experience a sense of isolation when they're not in contact with others; introverts experience the very same sense of isolation when they're in a crowd. Extroverts enjoy parties, meetings, discussion groups, and neighborhood gatherings; introverts may prefer solitary activities, individual sports, or relaxing in front of the television.[1] Needless to say, Sociability can be a great source of conflict between differently oriented partners.

Energy: The Need to Recharge

Energy is the question of what drains you and, when those mental and emotional fuel cells are depleted, what recharges you once again. Extroverts tend to recharge in social gatherings; people are an energy source to them. An extrovert may be the last one to leave the party, and when it's over she may go looking for another because she is rejuvenated by the experience.

But introverts tend to recharge alone; people are an energy *drain* to them. An introvert may be reluctant to attend the party at all, and once he's there he may count the minutes until he can leave again. It's not that he doesn't *like* parties; it's just that parties wear him out. People require Energy.

Mates require Energy too. Different approaches to Openness can cause marriage partners to disagree about the amount of time they should spend together. An extroverted spouse may feel rejected by her privacy-seeking partner. But as communication scholar Julia Wood reminds us, "There is nothing wrong when we seek privacy; it doesn't mean a relationship is in trouble. It means only that we need both openness and closedness in our lives."[2]

There's nothing wrong with being an introvert *or* an extrovert. However, extroverted husbands often marry introverted wives—and vice versa—and that's where the trouble begins. Imagine an introverted husband married to an extroverted wife. She values Sociability and draws Energy through interaction with others. Her husband, on the other hand, values privacy and prefers to recharge alone. They both return home after an exhausting day at work—how will they spend their evening?

In all likelihood, they will spend their evening arguing about Openness.

She: *I'd sure like to see that new movie . . .*
He: *Why don't you go? It's showing at 7:30.*
She: *Will you go with me?*
He: *That movie doesn't interest me. I'd rather finish my novel.*
She: *It's only two hours.*
He: *No thanks. I'd rather read.*

She: *Never mind then. I can't go by myself.*

He: *Why can't you go by yourself? It's just a movie. Even if you go with someone else, you just sit there.*

She: *That's not the point. I can't enjoy a movie by myself.*

He: *I thought the point was to see a movie, not have a party.*

Movie watching is a solitary activity—a roomful of strangers sitting side by side in individual seats, staring straight ahead at the screen without speaking a word. But a true extrovert will seek to turn even movie watching into a group event.

Because the woman in our scenario is an Open personality, two questions come to her mind simultaneously: "What movie will I see?" and "Whom will I see it with?" To her, it's unthinkable that she would attend a movie alone. What's the fun in that? *I can't enjoy a movie by myself.*

But her introverted husband thinks the point in going to a movie is to see a movie, just as the point in going bowling is to knock down pins. To him, the most important question is always, "What will we *do?*" To her, the really important question is, "Whom will we do it *with?*"

Will you go with me? she asks her husband, but the question he hears through his introvert's ears is, "Do you want to see this movie?" *I'd rather read,* he responds. Why would he want to see a movie he isn't interested in? To her the answer is obvious: "To be with *me.*"

He doesn't want to do an activity he isn't interested in, and she doesn't want to attend an activity alone. But there is one activity they do together—they both argue about Openness.

She 1:   *I think public schools give the kids much more exposure to different kinds of people.*

She 2:   *So do I, but it's hard to beat the quality of a private education. What do you think, honey?*

He: *What?*

She 2: *You weren't listening at all, were you?*

He: *Were you talking to me?*

She 2: *No, but we were talking, and you're sitting right here. You just tuned the whole thing out, didn't you?*

She 1: *My husband does the same thing. It's like he has his own little private world, and when nothing I'm saying interests him, he just disappears into it.*

She 2: *That's exactly what **he** does, and it drives me crazy because then I have to repeat everything.*

He: *What?*

While Open personalities value Sociability, introverts are more territorial—and the private territory they withdraw to is sometimes in the mind. Introverts have an internal world, and the seclusion of this private sanctuary is never more than a mental step away. When there's nothing interesting going on in the real world, introverts simply retreat into a world of their own.

These two women are having a conversation—not a conversation *with* the man, but a conversation right in *front* of him. But he's not interested in the topic, so he mentally checks out. When his wife finally asks him a direct question, they find his apartment vacated and his closet empty. *You weren't listening at all, were you?*

Extroverts have a hard time accepting this tendency or even understanding the capacity. How can you simply *tune out* a conversation that's going on right in front of you? To an extrovert, a conversation is a call to arms, an open invitation to participate. But an introvert doesn't want to expend his Energy on every fleeting exchange. The husband wants to know if this conversation involves *him*. *Were you talking to me?*

The introvert's approach to conversation is, "If you need me, call me." Otherwise, he'll be in a world of his own.

He: *This should be a great party. I've really been looking forward to this.*

She: *How long do we have to stay?*

He: *How long do we have to stay? We haven't even got there yet! Why did you agree to come if you already can't wait to leave?*

She: *I wanted to come. I just don't want to burn up the whole evening here.*

He: *Burn up the whole evening? What are you in such a rush to get home to, the TV? Talk about burning up a whole evening!*

She: *I just don't know anybody there.*

He: *That's the whole point of coming, to meet some new people.*

She: *I'm just not up for meeting new people tonight.*

He: *You're never up for meeting new people! You know, you are really getting dull.*

He's a party animal, and she's a party pooper. They haven't even arrived at the party yet, and already she's planning her exit. *Why did you agree to come if you already can't wait to leave?* But she *did* want to come—she likes parties too. But being an introvert, she has begun to take a mental inventory of the Energy it will require to greet strangers, smile incessantly, and engage in dialogue for the next three hours straight.

He doesn't understand her attitude. He thinks her negativity sucks the life out of every get-together. She seems to drag her feet wherever they go. *You know, you are really getting dull.* It's hard to understand because, for him, parties are *effortless.* You don't have to do anything; you just show up—and you always feel better when you leave. But she thinks about parties the way she thinks about going to the gym. It's good for her, and she likes to go, but it's going to *cost* her.

I just don't know anybody there, she complains. It takes

less Energy to interact with an intimate group of familiar friends than to break new ground with a roomful of perfect strangers. But to him, *That's the whole point of coming, to meet some new people.* Because he values Sociability, his boundaries are always expanding. For her, the path is narrow that leads to her door, and only a few at a time are welcomed in.

Neither one may enjoy the evening—not because the party was a flop, but because they don't have the same approach to Openness.

Different Needs for Social Contact

She: There's a new Sunday school class starting up. I think we should join it.

He: What's the topic?

She: It would be a great way to get to know some of the other couples in the church. The main service is so large now, I hardly even recognize anyone.

He: What would we be studying in this class?

She: I don't know. It sounds like a good opportunity. What do you think? Do you want to go?

He: How would I know? You don't even know what the class is about!

Because she values Sociability, she instinctively evaluates an event in terms of its potential for interaction, and a Sunday school class would be just the thing. That's all she needs to know; her decision is made. *It sounds like a good opportunity,* she says to her husband. *Do you want to go?* But to him, it's a Sunday school *class,* and a class has to be about something. *What would we be studying in this class?*

Because he doesn't always think in terms of Sociability, he sees no *purpose* yet for the class. Without a clear purpose to consider, how does he decide to attend or not? *How would I know?*

He thinks she's impulsive, and she thinks he's antisocial. Our different views of Openness can cause us to approach the same event from completely different directions.

She: I saw an interesting book today. It's called The Friendless American Male.

He: Oh?

She: I've been thinking . . . you really need some more friends.

He: Me? I've got all the friends I need.

She: Name one.

He: Well . . . there's Bob.

She: Bob? You call Bob a friend? You see him once every three months at a business convention. I'm not talking about casual acquaintances; I'm talking about real friends.

He: How about Jim? Jim's a friend.

She: Okay, so you've got one friend. But you need more than that.

He: Why?

She: Why? You don't understand why you need friends?

He: I don't understand why I need **more** *friends. One is enough for me.*

Everyone needs friends—but *how many* friends, and what *kind?* Our contrasting approaches to Openness cause us to answer those questions in very different ways.

She values Sociability, so she treasures friendship. She never has enough friends, and she's always eager to make a new one. Without her friends she would feel isolated, alienated, and disconnected.

She looks at her introverted husband and she sees a man who has no friends—a man who, therefore, must be isolated, alienated, and disconnected. Because she loves her husband, she wants to help. *You need some more friends,* she tells him, and she is dumbfounded by his reply: *I've got all the friends I need.*

How is that possible? No one has all the friends they need! She challenges him on the number and quality of his friend-ships. *I'm not talking about casual acquaintances; I'm talking about real friends.* Her friends meet regularly for coffee to discuss intimate details about life, love, and family. *His* friends meet once a year to compare hockey tickets. After careful cross-examination, the fact emerges that he has but one true friend. But somehow, that's enough for him.

She doesn't just want her husband to have more friends— she wants her husband to have *her* kind of friends—intimate companions who are numerous and near. She may think of her husband as disconnected, but he just approaches friendship in a different way. Because he has a different view of Openness, he will always prefer to have just one or two close friends.

He: *What a week! I'm exhausted.*

She: *Me too. I can't wait for the weekend.*

He: *I've got an idea. . . . Let's get the whole gang together on Saturday and head for the beach.*

She: *(Groan) I thought you said you were tired.*

He: *I am. I've been sitting in my cubicle, chained to my desk all week. This would be a great way to recharge!*

She: *But I spent the whole week doing employee reviews. I've been meeting with people for four straight days. I just want to be alone.*

He: *C'mon, you could stand one more day of people.*

She: *And you could stand one more day alone.*

He: *You know, you could be a little more flexible.*

They're both exhausted—they can agree on that. The weekend is coming, and with it the chance to rest and be refreshed. They both feel the need to restore their Energy, but they will seek to recharge in different ways—and that's when an Openness conflict can begin.

Relaxing at the beach sounds great to *both* of them—but he adds a little something to the suggestion that spoils it for her. *Let's get the whole gang together.* She lets out a groan. To her, relaxing at the beach and getting the whole gang together are mutually exclusive.

The man in this scenario is really not an extrovert—but he has been *sitting in his cubicle, chained to his desk all week.* And his wife is not normally an introvert; she has just been *meeting with people for four straight days.* Sometimes our circumstances and environment influence our approach to Sociability and Energy. Introverts can go stir crazy, and extroverts can get tired of people. A privacy-seeking husband may unexpectedly throw a shindig, and a party-animal wife may suddenly lock her door.

The side you take in an Openness conflict is not always predictable. Sometimes it all comes down to the kind of week you had.

Have Sociability and Energy been behind some of *your* recurring conflicts? Take the Openness Inventory to find out . . .

OPENNESS INVENTORY—*Sociability*	YOU	MATE
Who would like to have people remember his birthday with a party of some kind?		
Who would like to invite the new neighbors over for dessert?		
Who initiates most of the social events in the home?		
Who is more concerned about being included and liked?		
Who worries more about your children not having enough friends?		
Who is more eager to check the mail and answering machine for messages?		
Who is more embarrassed by standing alone at a party?		
Who stays in better touch with long-distance friends and relatives?		

OPENNESS INVENTORY—*Energy*	YOU	MATE
Who would prefer to talk through a project with others rather than work on it alone?		
Who feels encouraged and happy at the end of a party, and afterward is ready to talk about what everybody said?		
Who prefers to spend time off with other people?		
Who would rather talk about people than talk about tasks?		
Who still has more to discuss at the end of the day?		
Who likes to get the opinions of other people before making a final decision?		
Who would more likely shrivel up working alone in a cubicle?		

Finding the Root

On a scale from one to ten, how important is Openness to you? Place an X where you think you belong. Now put an O where you think your mate belongs.

Are there recurring arguments in your marriage that you think might be driven by the differences between you and your mate in the area of Openness? What are they about?

Do you think there is something from your past that makes your approach to Openness especially important to you? Have you ever discussed this with your mate?

Do you think there is something from your past that makes Openness especially *difficult* for you? Have you ever discussed this with your mate?

Do you think there is something happening in your life right now that could be reinforcing your approach to Openness?

CHAPTER NINE

CONNECTION

Communication and Decision Making

Tim: *Joy and I weren't married very long before we realized that we Connect in different ways. We used to have a lot of conversations that went like this . . .*

Joy: *"Did you have a nice phone call with your mom this afternoon?"*

Tim: *"Sure."*

Joy: *"How is she?"*

Tim: *"Fine."*

Joy: *"You weren't on the phone very long. How did she sound?"*

Tim: *"How did she **sound**? Uh . . . far away."*

Joy: *"I mean, did she sound happy, or sad, or tired—you know, how did she sound?"*

Tim: *"She sounded fine. By the way, who were you talking to on the phone all this time?"*

Joy: *"My parents."*

Tim: *"For an entire hour? What in the world did you talk about? I can't think of that much to say in a week!"*

Joy: *"I don't know. We just talk about things."*

Tim: *"I could never talk to my parents for an hour."*

Joy: *"Why not?"*

Tim: *"I run out of things to talk about after the first three minutes."*

Joy: *"You don't have to talk about world issues—just talk to them."*

Tim: *"But I have to talk to them about **something**. What would I talk about?"*

Joy: *"Different things."*

Tim: *"Like what?"*

Joy: *"I talked to **my** parents about all the new flowers and plants they just planted."*

Tim: *"Flowers and plants? How can you talk for a whole hour about plants?"*

Joy: *"I don't mind talking about flowers and plants because I'm talking to **them**. Besides, we talked about other things too. We talked about you and the kids, and my brother, and the neighbors, and the American Legion team, and my dad's paintings, and my mom visiting the shut-ins from church, and the deer that have been coming into the backyard, and their trip to Newfoundland, and their new car, and my old high school's football team, and the weather."*

Tim: *(Long pause) "I talked to my mom about the weather, too."*

Joy: *"Really? How is the weather there?"*

Tim: *"Fine."*

Communicating to Connect

When different kinds of computers have to communicate, it sometimes leads to problems. They may be running at different speeds, or they may be speaking a different language altogether. Entire corporations exist to help ensure that computers are able to converse. Unfortunately, the same level of technical support is not available to husbands and wives, who often experience precisely the same difficulty with *Connection.*

Here are some comments from couples who have difficulty finding a way to Connect . . .

- *I don't understand his lack of emotion in trials.*

- *I wish she would use less emotion and more facts.*

- *He seems too domineering because he thinks too quickly.*

- *I don't understand why she walks into a store and stops right at the entrance to talk.*

- *It takes me awhile to verbalize my feelings. I need time to process conflict and not feel like I have to rush through it when I'm not ready.*

- *I wish she understood that my words aren't forged in stone. I am just trying to find the words. I'm trying to find out what I feel.*

- *I don't understand why decisions can take so long and be so difficult to make.*

- *He doesn't understand my need to discuss an issue with more than one conversation and on more than one occasion!*

- *He tends to become frustrated easily if a solution is not immediately forthcoming, and he withdraws.*

- *I'm not necessarily out for a specific answer; I just want to dialogue about possible solutions.*

- *I wish he would be more aggressive and open instead of having to talk for two hours to get to his true feelings.*

Connection conflicts can begin about any topic at all, but they quickly shift from the *content* of the discussion to its *style.* The argument is no longer about what you're saying, but how you're saying it—or *not* saying it. A Connection conflict makes it difficult to hear what your mate is saying at all.

Conflicting Communication Styles

Connection problems arise when couples have different styles of *Communication* and *Decision Making.* Your *Communication* style is the *way* you seek to interact. Your style of interaction can be a bigger source of conflict than the actual words you choose. Unfortunately, couples are often completely unaware of the way they instinctively seek to Connect. Our natural style of Communication is one of our most persistent blind spots. Three pairs of conflicting Communication styles are common between married couples: *linear vs. circular, emotional vs. cognitive,* and *interactive vs. didactic.*

Conflicting Decision-Making Styles

Your *Decision-Making* style is the way you choose between options great and small, from an order at the drive-through to the purchase of a home. There are dozens of life-changing decisions that husbands and wives must make together and countless minor choices to be resolved each day. Great frustration can result when couples approach decisions along very different paths. As a result, many couples avoid making decisions together at all. They just divide major decisions between them—and then live with the anger and disappointment that results when one partner makes an undesirable choice. There are three pairs of conflicting Decision-Making styles that are common to couples: *decisive vs. tentative, intuitive vs. evidential,* and *final vs. open-ended.*

The Root of Other Conflicts

Connection problems are sometimes the most serious of the Seven Conflicts, because they may underlie the other six. Until we resolve our differences in style, it may be impossible to resolve our differences in substance. In the scenarios that follow, we'll illustrate each of the conflicting Communication and Decision-Making styles and give you a taste of the frustration and confusion they can produce—that is, if you don't know already.

Communication Styles

Linear vs. Circular Communicators

He: *Did you see Johnny's teacher today?*

She: *I stopped by the school about noon. I thought I'd never get there—the lunchtime traffic was unbelievable! There's a building site near there and . . .*

He: *What did the teacher say?*

She: *She said he'll have to stay after school tomorrow. Have you been in that school lately? It's practically falling apart. Some of the ceiling tiles are . . .*

He: *Why does he have to stay after?*

She: *I don't like the idea of him sitting alone in that dark old classroom. Why should he be the only one who . . .*

He: *WHY DOES HE HAVE TO STAY AFTER?*

He orders his thoughts carefully before he speaks and then presents his ideas in a clear, concise, and orderly fashion—and he expects his wife to do the same in return. But often she doesn't. To him, she seems to speak as she thinks, and she stops to explore detours and rabbit trails as she pleases on the road to her eventual conclusion. This is the tension between *linear vs. circular* styles of Communication.

To the linear communicator, the destination is the thing, and he wants to find the shortest path to the goal. To the circular communicator, the trip itself is what it's all about, and you might as well relax and enjoy the ride.

He wants a report on the meeting with Johnny's teacher. *I stopped by the school about noon,* she begins—then suddenly her focus shifts to lunchtime traffic and roadside construction. He brings her back to the subject, and she resumes her report once again—then her attention inexplicably jumps to the condition of the school building. His frustration is steadily growing. Will she *ever* land this plane?

Though he doesn't recognize it, each of her detours *does* have something to do with the topic. Lunchtime traffic and roadside construction *did* play a role in her visit with the teacher, and the crumbling school building is a part of her concern for her son. But that isn't what he wants to hear. He came to this conversation with a three-point outline in mind: *Did you see Johnny's teacher? What did the teacher say? Why does he have to stay after?*

Linear communicators cannot bear the seemingly pointless meanderings of their circular partners. They find them illogical, wasteful, and draining, and that's why linear communicators are always interrupting to edit, summarize, or speed the story along. They want the facts, ma'am, *just* the facts. But to circular communicators, their linear spouses seem impatient, uncaring, and rude. They don't care about what you want to say; they only care about what they want to hear. Circular communicators fear that once they give their linear partners the facts, they will totally tune them out since they now have all the information they wanted. Linear and circular communicators approach a discussion with different goals in mind: She wants *conversation*, but he only wants *information*.

They're both concerned about Johnny, but they're having trouble communicating about it. They have a bad Connection.

Emotional vs. Cognitive Communicators

> *She: Did you see the news? There was a major airline disaster today.*
>
> *He: Huh.*
>
> *She: Did you hear what I said?*

He: *You said there was an airline disaster.*

She: *That's right. Two hundred people were on board
and there were no survivors. Men, women, children
—whole families perished. The photos were awful!*

He: *Huh.*

She: *Is that all you can say? "Huh"?*

He: *Uh . . . that's bad.*

A major airline disaster. Think of the lives shattered, the careers ended, the families split apart; think of the men, women, and children lost; think of the fear, the panic, the final moments of agony. She shares this gut-wrenching horror with her husband, whose heart pours out in response . . . *Huh.*

This is the contrast between *emotional vs. cognitive* communicators. She responds to news of the catastrophe with passion, her thoughts and emotions combining to give a heartfelt and compassionate response. The news of the airline disaster is more than a fact to be comprehended; it's a tragedy to be *experienced.*

But he responds to the tragedy as he responds to *all* problems—he holds it at arm's length and studies it. He approaches the subject logically, factually, creeping cautiously up to the edge and peering over, always careful not to get sucked into the quicksand of surrounding emotion.

To her, emotion is part of her thinking. To him, emotion *interferes* with his thinking. She thinks and feels at virtually the same instant; he thinks first and feels later—sometimes *much* later. His cognitive style drives her crazy; she feels as if she's talking to a stenographer instead of another human being. *Is that all you can say?* From the depths of his soul comes, *Uh . . . that's bad.*

Emotional communicators find their cognitive partners cold, distant, and disconnected. Cognitive communicators think their compassionate mates are just overreacting. If she would just stop to *think* first, she might be able to keep things in *perspective . . .*

He kept the airline disaster at arm's length, but he may not find it as easy to do with the Connection conflict that's coming his way.

Interactive vs. Didactic Communicators

He: *Your folks called today. They bought one of those —*

She: *Bread makers?*

He: *That's right. They said that they—*

She: *Do they like it?*

He: *Yes, they said they like it. It has one of those—*

She: *Dough hooks?*

He: *No, one of those—*

She: *Delay timers? Those are really handy.*

He: *Would you let me finish a sentence?*

Some think of conversation like a formal dinner, where dishes are served to you one at a time and your only job is to keep your seat and wait. Others think of conversation as a buffet where you take what you want when you want it. These are the contrasting styles of *interactive vs. didactic* Communication.

Didactic communicators think of dialogue as a series of presentations: First *you* talk, then *I* talk. Conversations should operate according to democratic principles of justice and fair play. You speak your piece, you wait your turn, and it's never polite to interrupt. But interactive communicators recognize no such rules. To them, a conversation is a *group* activity. If you have a question, throw it in. If you have a comment, voice it— even if the other person happens to be *talking* at the time.

He begins a presentation. *Your folks called today. They bought one of those* . . . But he hesitates for a split second, and to his interactive wife, that sounds like an invitation to jump right in. *Bread makers?* She finishes the sentence for him. To an interactive communicator, that's just being helpful.

He begins again, and this time she interjects a question.

Next, she guesses at the ending of another partial sentence. She guesses wrong, so she tries again. She's having a wonderful time interacting, but he's finding it impossible to complete his presentation. *Would you let me finish a sentence?*

The husband thinks his wife is being rude and impatient. But she isn't trying to be rude; she sees her interactive style as a sign of genuine interest and enthusiasm. Conversations are never dull when she's around. By contrast, her didactic husband can seem formal, stuffy, and downright boring. He seems to be more interested in what *he* has to say than in what anyone has to say in reply. That doesn't sound like a conversation to her—it sounds more like a speech.

He wants to speak, and she wants to interact.

Decision-Making Styles

Decisive vs. Tentative Decision Makers

Here's another couple who's having trouble establishing a Connection.

> She: *So are we going to Disney World or Universal Studios?*
>
> He: *I like Disney World. But I also like Universal . . .*
>
> She: *We said Disney World was better for the kids.*
>
> He: *That's right, it is . . . I suppose.*
>
> She: *Then let's go for it!*
>
> He: *I just want to look at the brochures once more.*
>
> She: *You know, you are driving me nuts.*
>
> He: *Maybe we should look at Epcot too . . .*

It's vacation time, and they have to decide together on a getaway location. What will it be—Disney World or Universal Studios? There's a lot riding on this decision: the kids' enjoyment, their own satisfaction, the best use of their limited funds.

And when are they ever going to have a chance like this again? So many choices—and so many possible regrets.

Somehow, it's an easy decision for her. It's not that there's only one clear option—*either* choice would be fine for her. She just wants to *decide*. But her husband will agonize over this decision. Again and again he will consider all options while avoiding a final commitment. This is the difference between the *decisive vs. tentative* styles of Decision Making.

I like Disney World. But I also like Universal Studios, he waffles. This is not the first time they've had this discussion. *We said Disney World was better for the kids,* she reminds him. He offers the slightest hint of a possible decision: *That's right, it is . . . I suppose . . .* and she's on it like an attack dog. *Then let's go for it!*

Tentative Decision Makers tend to focus on the *outcome* of their choices. Is this the best thing we can do? Are there better options we've overlooked? Have we missed anything in our Decision-Making process? What will it cost us if our decision turns out to be the wrong one? With so much at stake, it's no wonder some Decision Makers have a hard time making a final choice.

But *decisive* Decision Makers tend to concentrate on the decision *itself*. For them, an unfinalized decision is like a half-finished project or an unmade bed. There's a sense of *completion* that comes with a final decision, and they want to get it done. Enough of this endless discussion; let's just *decide*, even if it means sacrificing money or quality.

This tentative husband and decisive wife are like two people on either side of a door—one is trying to hold it open while the other is trying to pull it shut. With that approach, they may be vacationing at home this year.

Intuitive vs. Evidential Decision Makers

> She: So what do you think? The Toyota or the Honda?
> He: The Toyota. Definitely.

140

She: Why?

He: I just have a feeling about this. Trust me.

She: I looked at Consumer Reports . . . they say the Honda has a better repair record. But then I checked the Blue Book, and the Toyota keeps its value better . . .

He: The Toyota. No doubt about it.

She: How can you be so sure?

He: My gut tells me. I'm never wrong about these things.

She: I'd feel a lot better if your gut would look at some evidence.

He thinks they should buy the Toyota. He's not *half*-certain, or *almost* sure—he knows. *The Toyota. Definitely.* But if you pressed him on the *source* of his confidence, he'd have a hard time telling you. This is not the first car he's purchased, and he has some knowledge of automobiles, but his certainty comes more from an inner feeling, an intuitive sense that tells him this is the right choice. *My gut tells me.*

But to his wife, the way to approach a major decision is by reading, researching, and gathering data. Never mind what your gut tells you; what do the *facts* say? She might consider listening to her gut too, but only after *her* gut has taken the time to consider some objective evidence. *I'm never wrong about these things,* her husband says. His wife remembers differently. Sometimes he *is* wrong about these things, but that's not enough to suppress his inner sense of confidence and conviction. These are the contrasting styles of *intuitive vs. evidential* Decision Makers.

Evidential Decision Makers approach decisions by looking *outward*. They know that an objective evaluation of all the available evidence will give them the greatest possible chance of making a good decision. But intuitive Decision Makers see this as unnecessary. They know that facts can be manipulated and research can be endless and exhausting. Ultimately, you still have to *decide*. What does your gut tell you?

Intuitive Decision Makers find an evidential approach to be tedious, boring, and redundant. But evidential Decision Makers, who lack that inner sense of confidence, find an intuitive approach to be subjective, superficial, and unreliable. When one partner won't trust her instincts and the other won't listen to reason, it can be hard to make a decision about anything.

Final vs. Open-ended Decision Makers

> *She:*   *I bought this blouse today. How do you like it?*
>
> *He:*   *I love it. It's perfect for you.*
>
> *She:*   *Do you really like it? It was on sale, 10 percent off.*
>
> *He:*   *Sounds like a good deal. You can't beat 10 percent off.*
>
> *She:*   *I wonder . . . I bought it at a department store, and sometimes they have bigger sales over at the outlet mall.*
>
> *He:*   *Look, you already bought the blouse, so forget about it. It's a done deal.*
>
> *She:*   *I'm just going to run over to the outlet mall and take a look.*

She made a purchase today, but not a *final* purchase. For her, decisions are seldom final—they're always open to reconsideration. Some people make an ultimate decision and then they never look back. But others are less certain about the choices they've made, and they like to revisit them from time to time to either regret or rejoice. These are the different styles of the *final vs. open-ended* Decision Makers.

She has every reason to think she made a good decision about her blouse. *It was on sale, 10 percent off.* Her husband agrees, and he looks for every opportunity to help solidify her decision. *I love it. It's perfect for you. You can't beat 10 percent off.* The decision is over, but to her it's not *final.* It's an open-ended event that needs to be revisited to make doubly sure that it was the best thing to do—even if that means continuing to shop for the blouse after the purchase has been made.

Think again about the three pairs of Decision-Making styles we've considered. The *decisive vs. tentative* styles affect the way we first approach a decision; the *intuitive vs. evidential* styles influence the way we make the decision itself; but the *final vs. open-ended* styles don't come into play until after a decision has already been made.

She once bought new curtains for the house; it took her a week to make the selection, and she revisited her decision for another month. He once bought a bass boat; it took him fifteen minutes, and he never thought about it again. It's not that he makes better decisions than his wife; it's just that he has a different attitude toward the decisions he makes. For her, a decision is always open-ended. For him, all sales are final.

Even couples who agree on their decisions may not agree about their feelings after the choice has been made. Before, during, and after a decision, it's better if you can make a Connection.

Once again it's time to consider how this issue relates to you. What is your natural style of Communication and Decision Making? Take the following Connection Inventory to help decide . . .

CONNECTION INVENTORY— *Communication Style*	YOU	MATE
Who is more eager to get to the point without a lot of detail?		
Who finds it more difficult or tedious to make conversation if it isn't about an issue or task that interests her?		
Who has more trouble thinking of questions to ask and then genuinely listening to the answers?		
Who is quicker to try to fix a situation after hearing the problem?		
Who would rather deal with facts than emotions?		
Who gets more frustrated if the details of a story are not clear and accurate?		

CONNECTION INVENTORY— *Decision-Making Style*	YOU	MATE
Who makes decisions faster?		
Who feels the need to look at more options before making a decision?		
Who seems more confident after the decision has been made and feels fewer regrets?		
Who feels less of a need to look at research and other information before making a decision?		
Who sometimes makes a decision without even consulting his mate?		
Who is less likely to agonize over major decisions?		
Who would rather make a decision for the sake of convenience, preferring to save time rather than find the highest quality or the best deal?		

Finding the Root

What is your natural Communication style? Place an X on each continuum where you think you belong. Then place an O where you think your mate belongs.

←————————————————————————→
linear   circular

←————————————————————————→
emotional   cognitive

←————————————————————————→
interactive   didactic

What is your natural Decision-Making style? Place an X on each continuum where you think you belong. Then place an O where you think your mate belongs.

←————————————————————————→
decisive   tentative

←————————————————————————→
intuitive   evidential

←————————————————————————→
final   open-ended

Are there recurring arguments in your marriage that you think are the direct result of poor Connection? What are they about?

Do you think there is something from your past that makes your desire for quality Connection especially important to you? Have you ever discussed this with your mate?

Do you think there is something from your past that makes Connection especially *difficult* for you? Have you ever discussed this with your mate?

Do you think there is something happening in your life right now that could be heightening your desire for better Connection?

QUICK take

For Chapters 3 through 9

S even common underlying issues are the root causes of most of the conflicts in married life: *Security, Loyalty, Responsibility, Caring, Order, Openness,* and *Connection.*

Security is the need to be safe, the desire to know that you and yours are first of all protected from harm. There are two chief components of Security: the desire for *Protection* and the desire for *Provision. Protection* in its most basic form is the instinct for survival, but it also includes the longing for safety, stability, and even comfort. *Provision* is the desire to make sure everyone has enough, a desire that makes it necessary to both collect and save.

Because Security looks to the future, it would rather save than spend; because Security wants to provide, it would rather collect than throw away; because Security wants to protect, it has an aversion to risk.

If Security is not your natural priority, your Security-minded partner can seem like a killjoy. Why can't he lighten up? But if Security *is* your priority, then your risk-taking partner seems just plain irresponsible. After all, it's *safety* we're talking about here, and surely that comes before everything else.

We often fail to recognize the Security issue because it comes to us in the form of a dozen smaller, seemingly unrelated arguments—disagreements about money, and irresponsibility, and overprotecting the kids. But underneath it all is the issue of Security.

Loyalty is the dream of a mate who is unreservedly committed to you and to the relationship. Loyalty has two essential elements: *Faithfulness* and *Priority*. *Faithfulness* means being able to count on someone regardless of the issue and regardless of the circumstances. Faithfulness is what we vow first and foremost on our wedding day. *Priority* is something else we vow on our wedding day. Priority is what we mean by the phrase "forsaking all others." It means to move someone new into first place in your life. In the case of marriage, it means to put someone in her *rightful* place.

Each of us is born with an instinctive "me first" attitude. But in marriage, every husband and wife has to cultivate a *"we first"* mentality—and each needs to know that his or her partner shares that value. We all need to know that the marriage will come before the in-laws, the best friends, even the children.

Each of us desires our spouse to be faithful in the most basic sense, but the dream of Loyalty goes much deeper. Unseen aspects of Faithfulness and Priority cause conflict in day-to-day married life. Arguments about the role of the in-laws, the priority of the children, a husband's wandering eyes, and the amount of time spent at work and home are common examples of Loyalty conflicts.

Responsibility begins with the word *ought:* We *ought* to do this; we *ought* to take care of that. In marriage, one partner often has a greater sense of duty to follow the dictates of laws, customs, fashions, and the expectations of others. There are two components of the value of Responsibility: *Obligation* and *Expectation*. *Obligation* is an internal sense of what is *owed*. Every culture has thousands of unwritten customs and mores —things we're told we *ought* to do, but each of us has a different sense of just how important it really is to comply. That inner sense of *oughtness* is what we call Obligation. *Expectation* is your idea of what other people require of you. What do the neighbors expect of me? What do others think I should do? Expectation asks the question, "What will people think?"

149

All of us are governed by some internal sense of Obligation and Expectation, but we don't always agree on what the rules are or how important it is that we obey them. This difference in internal value systems is what creates the Responsibility conflict, which often begins over issues like the upkeep of the house, obeying traffic laws, and social or family obligations.

Caring literally means "feeling and exhibiting concern and empathy for others." It's a great source of encouragement when someone is willing to Care—and a common source of conflict when he is not. There are two components of Caring, and one flows from the other like a river from a stream. The stream is *Awareness,* and the river it produces is *Initiative. Awareness* is mental and emotional alertness, an attitude of attentiveness to your mate's feelings and concerns. Initiative is what flows naturally from Awareness. *Initiative* is the willingness to engage your mate about a problem once you've become aware of it. It's encouraging to know that your mate is at least conscious of your concern, but it means a lot more when he's willing to *do* something about it.

Concerns about a lack of Caring are voiced far more often by women than men. Women complain that their husbands are not aware and they do not initiate—and this is the beginning of the Caring conflict. Caring conflicts underlie many common disagreements: the failure to notice your mate's appearance, a lack of initiative on behalf of the kids, an unwillingness to deal with the messiness of your mate's emotions, and a failure to voice appreciation. All these issues have their roots in the issue of Caring.

Order is the desire to have things organized, orderly, and predictable. Some people want things to go according to plan. They like to know where everything is, and they want to know what comes next. But others would rather take life as it comes. They prefer things spontaneous, unexpected, and unpredictable. As life becomes more complex, Order becomes a critical issue and a source of great frustration for married couples.

There are two aspects of Order: the desire for *Structure* and the desire for *Control*. *Structure* is the dream of having a place for everything and everything in its place, but it's much more than that. The desire for Structure can extend not only to household organization, but also to time, work, hobbies, shopping, leisure, and even sex. The underlying conviction is that *anything works better with a plan*. *Control* is the desire to somehow keep a firm grip on the steering wheel of life. It's an uncertain world. How can you increase your chances of success? By maintaining Control. And what better way to maintain Control than through forethought, planning, and discipline? If things are in Order, they're under Control—at least the odds seem more in your favor.

Order conflicts may begin about household organization, personal records, punctuality, or the way you spend your leisure time, but they ultimately reduce to the underlying desires for Structure and Control.

Openness has to do with your attitude toward people and your need for privacy. Do groups of people invigorate you, or are your batteries drained by social interaction? Where do you instinctively go when you need to *recharge*—do you seek the company of others, or do you search for some space of your own?

Openness has two chief components: *Sociability* and *Energy. Sociability* is the desire to be with other people, an orientation that finds its greatest fulfillment through connection with others. Sociable personalities are traditionally referred to as *extroverts,* while their privacy-seeking counterparts are known as *introverts. Energy* is the question of what drains you, and, when those mental and emotional fuel cells are depleted, what recharges you once again. Extroverts tend to recharge in social gatherings; people are an energy *source* to

151

them. But introverts tend to recharge alone; people are an energy *drain* to them.

There's nothing wrong with being an introvert *or* an extrovert. But extroverted husbands often marry introverted wives—and vice versa—and that's where the trouble begins. Openness conflicts can start over anything where people are concerned, like social functions, time spent together vs. time spent alone, the priority of friendships, and the use of leisure time.

Connection problems arise when couples have different styles of *Communication* and *Decision Making*. Your *Communication* style is the *way* you seek to interact. Your style of interaction can be a bigger source of conflict than the actual words you choose. Unfortunately, couples are often completely unaware of the way they instinctively seek to Connect. Three pairs of conflicting Communication styles are common between married couples: *linear vs. circular, emotional vs. cognitive,* and *interactive vs. didactic.*

Your *Decision-Making* style is the way you choose between options. There are dozens of life-changing decisions that husbands and wives must make together, and great frustration can result when couples approach decisions along very different paths. Three pairs of conflicting Decision-Making styles are common to couples: *decisive vs. tentative, intuitive vs. evidential,* and *final vs. open-ended.*

Connection conflicts can begin about any topic at all, but quickly shift from the *content* of the discussion to its *style.* The argument is no longer about what you're saying, but how you're saying it—or *not* saying it. A Connection conflict makes it difficult to hear what your mate is saying at all. Connection problems are sometimes the most serious of the Seven Conflicts, because they may underlie the other six. Until we resolve our differences in style, it may be impossible to resolve our differences in substance.

To *really* understand the Seven Conflicts, you might want to go back and read about each of them in detail. And don't forget to do the Inventories at the end of each chapter—that will help you understand how each of the Seven Conflicts relates to *your* marriage.

In the next chapter we'll encourage you to reconsider your ideas about marriage itself and the necessary role that conflict plays in it. You can read about it in chapter 10 or in the Quick Take that follows.

part three

*Resolving
the Seven Conflicts*

CHAPTER TEN

WHAT ARE WE FIGHTING FOR?

W hen we were doing the original research for this book, we interviewed scores of couples about the topics they most often disagreed about in their marriage. We found ourselves having a recurring conversation that went something like this:

Us: *Tell us about the things in your marriage that you seem to argue about over and over again.*

She: *We don't argue in our marriage.*

He: *No, we don't. Not really.*

Us: *Oh. Okay . . . Do you agree about everything?*

She: *Oh, no, we disagree about things.*

He: *We just don't argue. (He takes her hand and they smile at each other.)*

She: *Like when he gets ready for church, he gets in the car and pulls out in the driveway and waits for me to come out. (She laughs.)*

He: *I guess we do disagree about that. (He laughs too.) I just think you should respect other people's time. When she makes me wait, it's like she's saying, "Your time is unimportant, so you can wait for me."*

She: *(Dropping his hand) If you'd help get the kids ready, instead of sitting in the car testing out the horn, we might be ready sooner.*

He: *So it's the kids' fault? So why does this happen even when the kids aren't around? What's your excuse then?*

Us: *(Taking notes furiously) Please tell us more about the way you don't argue.*

We Never Argue

Our research has taught us that just as prisons are filled with innocent men, Christian marriages are filled with couples who never argue. Of course, they *disagree* from time to time; they may differ, or squabble, or bicker, or even have a tiff—but they definitely do not argue. We found Christian couples to be a walking thesaurus when it comes to "arguing." They seem to do everything else *but.*

You might be interested to know that *The Seven Conflicts* was not the original title of this book. We intended to call it *The Seven Arguments of Marriage.* We thought that title was clear, to the point, and did a good job of communicating at a glance what the book is all about. But the publisher flatly rejected it because of the word *argument.* They told us that there is a strange ambivalence among readers toward the entire topic of "marital conflict." It seems that on the one hand readers are eager to learn how to argue less, while at the same time they don't want to admit that they argue at all. Why do Christians have this strange reluctance to admit that we actually argue from time to time? Not just differ, or disagree, or diverge, but *argue.*

We have spoken at weekend marriage conferences for almost twenty years now, with audiences that range from a few hundred to the thousands. When we come to the topic of "resolving conflict," we always tell our audience that the problem with marriage is that it's so isolated. None of us has any idea what's really going on behind another couple's closed doors—yet we're somehow sure they're doing better than we are. We're tortured by a mental image of the Perfect Couple, the couple who never argues. There they are, over in the corner—the ones sitting so close they could pass for Siamese twins. Wait—there they are, by the doorway—the ones smiling as if they're sitting in a lukewarm bath. I'll bet they never fight. I'll bet their entire marriage is one long, passionate, romantic getaway . . .

The irony, of course, is that those same couples are looking at you, imagining how perfect your marriage must be. Surely *you* never argue . . .

That's why we always ask the couples in our audience to pick out a couple—any couple will do—turn to them, and say, "We fight too." No one ever hesitates; in fact, sometimes we have trouble getting the audience under control again. What a catharsis! What an incredible sense of relief just to hear someone else say it! By the way, we always take part in this little exercise too. We tell the audience, "If you think it's embarrassing to have a fight on the way to attend a marriage conference, you should try having a fight on the way to *speak* at a marriage conference."

We have discovered that the very presence of conflict in marriage is a source of embarrassment and even shame for Christians. Don't misunderstand us—we've all had disagreements in our marriages that we *should* be ashamed of, because of their style or intensity or because of the foolish and hurtful things we did or said. But we have found that Christians are often ashamed that conflict is there at all, regardless of how it's handled. Christians tend to see conflict as fundamentally incompatible with romantic love, commitment, and spiritual maturity. Arguing seems to have no place in a truly Christian marriage. The ideal marriage is thought to have no conflict at all.

This commonly held conviction only deepens with the passage of time. It's natural that we should disagree from time to time when we're first married, but surely we should have worked this out by *now*. The only possible explanation for our ongoing disagreement is sin, or stubbornness, or maybe even a fundamental weakness in the marriage itself. Maybe we were never right for each other at all.

The purpose of this chapter is to encourage you to consider an entirely new attitude toward conflict in marriage. Yes, we all argue at times in inappropriate ways, and yes, we could all stand to reduce the amount of conflict in our marriages—but we want you to consider a different attitude toward conflict *itself*. We cannot emphasize enough the importance of this first step. This is far more than trying to apply the "power of positive thinking" or trying to see a half-empty glass as half-full. *This is an attempt to re-understand what marriage is supposed to be and the necessary role that conflict plays in it.*

Why is this step so important? If we view conflict only as a negative activity, as never more than the manifestation of sinfulness or selfishness or pride, then our response to conflict when it occurs will be negative. We'll seek to deny it, ignore it, or run from it—anything to make it just go away. And in fact, this is precisely what most of us do. Researchers agree that the most common ways couples deal with marital conflict are through conquest, avoidance, bargaining, and the quick fix.

But how are we supposed to take on a new attitude toward conflict? How do we begin to think in a positive way about something that's been such a source of anger, frustration, and regret? We might as well have called this chapter "The Stomach Flu: Give It Another Chance," or "Satan: Not Such a Bad Guy After All." How do we learn to accept the unacceptable?

Rethinking Conflict in Marriage

The place to begin is not by focusing on conflict itself, but by stepping back and taking a fresh look at marriage itself. We'd like you to consider five revolutionary ideas—thoroughly biblical ideas—that can change the way you look at conflict in your marriage.

God Is Not Finished with You Yet

Back in the 1960s, that fabled era of free spirits and free love, there was a poster that we used to see all the time. To fully appreciate it, try to imagine it glowing under a black light with the smell of incense smoldering in the background.

I am not on this earth to change you,
And you are not on this earth to change me.
But if our paths should cross
And our lives should touch,
It is beautiful.

It almost makes you want to tie-dye your T-shirt and wear a headband, doesn't it? At first reading it sounds noble and even a little profound, but it's hard to imagine a more unbiblical sentiment—especially for married couples. For those of us who have entered the covenant of marriage, there should be a poster more like this:

I am on this earth to change you,
And you are on this earth to change me—
Not by criticizing or demanding,
But by seeking to truly know and love each other.
If we spend the next thirty, forty, or fifty years together
And are not better human beings because of it,
May God forgive us both.

How does our little poster strike you? It isn't destined to become a best-seller, that's for sure, because it flies in the face of a common understanding of *tolerance*. According to some, no human being is qualified to change the life of another. But according to the Bible, *no human being is qualified to remain as he is.*

161

The Bible tells us that though God loves us, He is not yet *finished* with us—any more than we are finished with our own children. We love our kids, and we accept them for who they are, but we still want them to mature and grow in a hundred different ways. We're not always sure what the finished product should look like, but we're sure of what we *don't* see. It isn't hard to see that our children, no matter what their ages, still have a lot of growing up to do. God wants the same for us. Maybe that's why it has been said, "Marriage is the last chance God gives you to grow up." God wants us to grow, too, regardless of our ages—and He has a very clear picture of what the finished product should look like. We are to grow to look more and more like His own Son—like God Himself in human form—and marriage plays a tremendous role in this growth process.

Dan Allender and Tremper Longman, in their excellent book *Intimate Allies,* write:

> Marriages can become plodding, cyclical routines filled with boredom and obligation. No one expects that a marriage will retain the giddy glow of excitement that comes with the novelty of new love. But it is equally wrong to assume that passion must wane simply because of familiarity. True passion comes from the nature of the purpose of a marriage.[1]

Marriage sometimes becomes a boring routine—but it doesn't have to. Contrary to popular opinion, it's possible for a couple to share passion even after years of married life. By "passion" we mean much more than simply sexual desire. Passion is the consuming fire of life. Think of it as enthusiasm, or eagerness, or *gusto*—an ancient Italian word that means "a taste for life." *Passion* is perhaps the one word we would most like to describe our lives—and our marriages too. But where does passion come from? In marriage, passion comes from a clear understanding of what marriage is *for.*

"The purpose of every marriage," Allender and Longman write, "is to shape the raw material of life to reveal more fully the glory of God."[2] And just what are the "raw materials" that marriage is intended to shape? First and foremost, those raw materials are *you* and *your mate*.

> Our greatest privilege is not in shaping a symphony, learning to fly-fish, directing a ministry, or even providing food and clothing for our children. Our greatest privilege is shaping the character of the soul to reflect the image of Christ.
>
> We are to invite one another to become more like our God.[3]

The view that we should be willing to be changed by our partner is viewed by many as intolerant—but the view that we should be *unwilling* to be changed by one another is viewed by the Bible as supremely *arrogant*. God loves us, and He will never leave us—but He will never leave us *alone*, either. He is not finished with us yet.

Marriage Is One of the Tools God Uses to Shape Us

One of the questions we like to ask at marriage conferences is, "What do you think marriage is *for*?" We get a lot of blank stares when we ask that one, as if we were asking, "What are legs for?" or "Why should you breathe?" It's a question that doesn't seem to *need* an answer. Marriage isn't really *for* anything, is it? We marry for the same reasons we climb a mountain—because it's *there*.

Actually, "What is marriage for?" is a critical question. Your answer to that question would tell us a lot about your level of satisfaction with your marriage. It's a question of expectations. What we're really asking is, "What did you *expect* marriage to be?" Some of us expected marriage to be like an endless date, or like a forty-year love affair, or like a long bike ride coasting downhill with the wind in our hair . . .

Some of us were seriously disappointed.

"What is marriage for?" is a question most couples never ask, yet they have an answer for it nonetheless—an implicit answer. Most couples assume that marriage, like life itself, is to *enjoy*. If the purpose of marriage is simply to maximize our pleasure, then if we aren't enjoying ourselves, something is wrong. If marriage is to enjoy, then when we come to a difficult decision, the only relevant question is, "What would please me most?"

And if marriage is only to enjoy, whatever *isn't* pleasurable is an enemy of the marriage—something to be endured, or tolerated, or better yet avoided altogether. Conflict, it goes without saying, is rarely a barrel of fun.

Imagine a mental dialogue with the average pleasure-seeking husband or wife. The conversation might go something like this:

Q: *What is marriage for?*

A: *Marriage is to make life more enjoyable.*

Q: *Then what is conflict?*

A: *Conflict is when we're not getting along. It's an interruption in our enjoyment of marriage and of each other.*

Q: *Then how do you respond to conflict?*

A: *You do whatever you have to do to get back to enjoying each other.*

The Bible's most revolutionary teaching on the subject of marriage is not about roles, or commitment, or communication; the Bible's most profound insight is that *there is a purpose for marriage*. The purpose of marriage is to glorify God by helping to reshape each of us into the person he or she is intended to be.

As philosopher and psychologist Thomas Moore puts it, "Marriage may look like an arrangement of persons, but at a deeper level it is a profound stirring of souls."[4] There is far more to marriage than meets the eye. It may look like a simple living arrangement or social contract, but as Moore says, at a deeper level "it is the creation of a vessel in which soul-making can be accomplished."[5]

Marriage, in other words, is a kind of workshop. It is a woodshop where warped and curling timbers are flattened and splintered surfaces are sanded smooth. It is an auto shop where twisted frames are straightened and crumpled dents are pulled out and filled. It is a blacksmith shop where hammers clang and sparks fly and the hardest of metals are slowly willed into useful shapes. Marriage is the place where we are hammered, molded, and loved into the image of Christ.

If we could have a mental dialogue about marriage with the authors of Scripture, it might go something like this:

Q: *What is marriage for?*

A: *Marriage is intended to glorify God by helping to reshape each of us into the person God intended him to be.*

Q: *Then what is conflict?*

A: *Conflict is often a clash of passions. As iron sharpens iron, so one man sharpens another. Conflict is a tool in the sharpening process.*

Q: *Then how do you respond to conflict?*

A: *By asking, "What am I supposed to learn from this about myself, my Creator, and my mate?"*

In case it has been a few years since you were in a classroom, allow us to remind you: *Learning isn't always fun.* Learning *is* a lot of fun when you're first getting started—then it's all Big Bird and Crayolas and Hukd on Fonix. But the older you get, the harder the lessons become, and learning requires more discipline and repetition and sometimes a whole lot of caffeine.

The lessons of marriage are no different. "Education isn't a preparation for life," John Dewey once said; "education *is* life."

Marriage Will Not Always Be Enjoyable

Workshops are dangerous places with the potential for serious injury. Marriage is no different. Any tool sharp enough to smooth and shape can also rip and wound. Marriage is the ultimate intimacy workshop, and the potential for hurt is very real.

> Marriage brings together two people who are created in the image of God. They individually and as a couple reflect divine glory. Marriage is an awesome and wonderful union that has great potential for joy and celebration.
>
> The Bible, though, is a realistic book. It also describes us as flawed, selfish creatures; we are sinners. When two sinners come together, they do not become less selfish or less flawed; they become more so. Marriage is a frightening prospect that can be the arena for harm and pain.[6]

But if marriage is a workshop that can sometimes be an "arena for harm and pain," how are we to protect ourselves? You can avoid the workshop altogether and greatly reduce your risk of injury, just as you can avoid the kitchen and reduce your risk of eating. To refuse to enter the workshop of marriage, which many married couples do, is to refuse to be educated—to refuse to *grow*. Skip the workshop, and you miss what marriage is *for*. No pain—but no gain.

If "Woodshop 101" is not an elective but a required course, then how *do* we protect ourselves from injury? Simply put, *by learning to use the tools properly*. As in all workshops, the greatest risk of danger is not from using the tools, but from *misusing* them. The workshop is not a place to be careless. In chapters 11 through 14 we'll equip you in the use of a series of power tools that every marital workshop should possess and every married person should master.

We Will Sometimes Resent the Role
Our Mate Plays in This Shaping Process

An unpolished gemstone looks no different than an ordinary piece of gravel. To polish it, you need three things: a rock tumbler, some abrasive grit, and at least one other stone. A rock tumbler is little more than a jar lying on its side atop a series of rollers. A motor powers the rollers; when you turn the tumbler on, the jar begins to roll, and whatever is inside the jar begins to—you guessed it—*tumble.*

Inside the jar you place the stones and some abrasive grit. When the tumbler begins to roll, the rocks will slowly rise up the wall of the jar and then drop, crashing into one another, over and over again. Each time they collide, the grit removes a tiny bit of surface material at the point of impact. Each time they collide the stones become a little smoother—very, very slowly.

What happens if you forget the abrasive grit? The stones will still collide, but without an abrasive there's nothing to *smooth* the stones. They'll continue to crash into each other—perhaps even chip or damage each other—but the finished product will look no smoother than it did when you began. Thousands of impacts, but no polish.

And what happens if you forget the other stone? Absolutely nothing. The lone rock will still tumble, but with nothing to strike *against,* it simply rises and falls. There will still be some abrasion as the stone bounces against the side of the jar, but without another stone—without something of equal hardness to strike against—the polishing process could take years instead of weeks.

It isn't exactly enjoyable to be the other rock in someone else's tumbler. It isn't pleasant to collide with your mate—whether it's over Security, or Loyalty, or Caring, or Connection—and it's even less pleasant when your mate crashes into *you.* But that's the growth process of marriage; God drops two stones of equal hardness into the tumbler of marriage, and *He Himself is the abrasive.* With His help we smooth and polish one another; without Him, we only collide.

This is the strange paradox of marriage. We assume that growth is occurring when everything is going well in marriage, and that conflict always represents a step backward. In fact, it's often just the opposite; we not only grow *despite* our conflicts, but we also grow *because* of them. "Marriage is an institution of joy and grief," Allender and Longman write. "And the glory often comes through the struggles in communication, goals, priorities, child rearing, and sex. Anyone who expects glory without a fight is foolish."[7]

No one likes to cause friction, but it's a necessary part of the smoothing process. We need to accept the role that our mate is sometimes called to play in our lives, and we need to embrace the process itself. "Faithful are the wounds of a friend," Proverbs 27:6 tells us, and sometimes a wound is the most faithful thing your mate can give.

The Presence of Conflict in Your Marriage Means Nothing

If marriage is for the purpose of molding us into the image of Christ, and if conflict is a necessary part of that process, then it follows that conflict itself is nothing to be ashamed of. But we do *not* mean to suggest that all conflict is a good and acceptable part of marriage! The worst thing we could do is to simply put a gloss over selfish, cruel, and even violent behavior. Our goal in this chapter is to challenge you to change your thinking about conflict *itself,* not to encourage you to glibly accept any and all forms of behavior from your mate. As we said before, any tool sharp enough to smooth and shape can also rip and wound, and conflict—*badly handled* conflict—can be an extremely destructive force. The presence of conflict in your marriage means nothing, but the way you conduct yourself in conflict means everything—because the way you and your mate deal with conflict determines whether you will grow from it or be wounded by it.

In the chapters that follow, we will turn our focus to the way to deal with the seven toughest conflicts in marriage. But before we proceed, we need to do a final mental checkup. Have you begun to change your attitude toward conflict in marriage? Remember what we said at the beginning of this chapter: *We cannot emphasize enough the importance of this first step—the attempt to re-understand what marriage is supposed to be and the necessary role that conflict plays in it.*

The messages we tell ourselves have the power to affect everything we are and do. If we tell ourselves that the only purpose of marriage is personal fulfillment, then we will view all unfulfilling elements of the marriage as hindrances to that goal. When conflict arises—unfulfilling as it tends to be—we will deal with it just as we would a flat tire, a broken window, a nagging headache, or an annoying telemarketer: We will do as little as is necessary to make it go away and then return as quickly as possible to the real business of pleasure.

But what if we begin to tell ourselves a *different message?* What if we begin to believe that marriage is actually *for* something, that its purpose is to help reshape us into the people God intends us to be, and that conflict can play a positive role in that process? As our thinking changes, so will we. We will begin to respond to conflict just as we would physical exercise, or study, or practicing a musical instrument. We will become students of conflict rather than avoiders; we will begin to wade into the confusion instead of simply giving up; and we will be willing to endure the occasional collisions for the sake of the polishing that we know is taking place.

What do *you* think?

the very presence of conflict in marriage is a source of embarrassment and even shame for Christian people. Christians tend to see conflict as fundamentally incompatible with romantic love, commitment, and spiritual maturity. Arguing seems to have no place in a truly Christian marriage, and if we *do* have conflict, something must be wrong with us. Surely we should have worked this out by *now.*

We want to encourage you to consider an entirely new attitude toward conflict in marriage. Yes, we all argue at times in inappropriate ways, and yes, we could all stand to reduce the amount of conflict in our marriages—but we want you to consider a different attitude toward conflict *itself.* We need to re-understand what marriage is supposed to be and the necessary role that conflict plays in it. We'd like you to consider five revolutionary ideas—thoroughly biblical ideas—that can change the way you look at conflict in your marriage.

1. God is not finished with you yet. God loves you, but He is not finished with you. He wants you to grow to look more and more like His own Son, and marriage plays a tremendous role in this growth process.

2. Marriage is one of the tools God uses to shape us into the people He wants us to be. The Bible's most profound insight on marriage is that *there is a purpose for marriage,* and it isn't simply for our personal enjoyment. The purpose of marriage is to glorify God by helping to reshape each of us into the person he or she is intended to be. That means marriage is a kind of workshop, and sometimes the sparks will fly.

3. Marriage will not always be enjoyable. Workshops are dangerous places, and marriage is no different. Marriage is the ultimate intimacy workshop, and the potential for hurt is very real. That's why we have to learn to handle the tools of conflict properly. The workshop is no place to be careless.

4. We will sometimes resent the role our mate plays in this shaping process. There is a strange paradox in marriage. We assume that growth is occurring only when everything is going well, and that conflict always represents a step backward. In fact, it's often just the opposite; we not only grow *despite* our conflicts, but we also grow *because* of them. We need to accept the role that our mate is sometimes called to play in our lives, and we need to embrace the process itself.

5. The presence of conflict in your marriage means nothing; the way you deal with conflict means everything. Conflict itself is nothing to be ashamed of, but we do *not* mean to suggest that all conflict is a good and acceptable part of marriage! The worst thing we could do is to simply put a gloss over selfish, cruel, and even violent behavior. Any tool sharp enough to smooth and shape can also rip and wound, and conflict—*badly handled* conflict—can be an extremely destructive force. The presence of conflict in your marriage means nothing, but the way you conduct yourself in conflict means everything—because the way you deal with conflict determines whether you will grow from it or be wounded by it.

In the next two chapters we'll describe five preliminary steps that are crucial to handling conflict well. You can read all about them in chapters 11 and 12, or you can read the Quick Take that immediately follows.

CHAPTER ELEVEN

taking the first steps

few things are so challenging as mastering the perfect golf swing, as thousands of avid golfers can testify. These seekers of perfection invest countless hours at the driving range rehearsing the fundamentals of grip, stance, addressing the ball, hip rotation, and proper follow through. Yet strangely, golfers rarely focus on what may be the most crucial element of all.

PGA Tour professional and commentator Bobby Clampett claims that, for the professional, the most critical element of the swing is what immediately *precedes* it—the backswing. Why is the backswing so important? The swing itself happens so fast, Clampett says, that the human mind is incapable of making significant corrections once the swing is under way. The swing, in other words, is little more than an extension of what comes before it. If the backswing is done properly, the swing that follows will be straight and true; but if the backswing is faulty, there's no time to correct for it later. The lesson to be learned: In golf, as in life, the game is sometimes over before we're even aware that it has begun.

This lesson especially applies to resolving conflict in marriage. The most crucial element is what *precedes* the disagreement. There is a kind of "backswing" in conflict resolution, too, and just as in golf, couples rarely pay attention to it. But just as in golf, a conflict is little more than an extension of what comes before it. If we take the time to focus on the steps leading up to a conflict, we greatly increase our chances of a peaceful and mutually satisfying follow-through. And if we fail to think about these five preliminary steps, once a conflict is under way, things happen much too quickly to correct for mistakes we made going in.

Step 1: Become an Ambassador of Goodwill

The most critical step is also the simplest. It begins by asking the honest question, "Do I really *want* to resolve this conflict?" Think carefully before you reply—the answer is not as obvious as it seems. Sometimes marital conflict is motivated by sheer *meanness*—the desire to punish, or wound, or get even for some past offense. "There is one who speaks rashly like the thrusts of a sword," Proverbs 12:18 says, and marriage makes master swordsmen of us all. Our conflicts are filled with sarcasm, criticism, blame, and contempt, and then we wonder why we don't seem to get anywhere. Is it any surprise? After all, how far would we get if we spoke that way to a stranger?

John Gottman, in his book *The Seven Principles for Making Marriage Work,* writes:

> To a certain degree, [solving problems] comes down to having good manners. It means treating your spouse with the same respect you offer to company. If a guest leaves an umbrella, we say, "Here. You forgot your umbrella." We would never think of saying, "What's wrong with you? You are constantly forgetting things. Be a little more thoughtful! What am I, your slave to go picking up after you?" We are sensitive to the guest's feelings, even if things don't go well. . . . What's really being asked of you is no more than would be asked if you were dealing with an acquaintance, much less the person who has vowed to share his or her life with you.[1]

All that's being asked of us, Gottman says, is *good manners* —the same sort of patience and kindness and understanding we would extend to anyone. But as we all know, sometimes it's more difficult to display those manners to the one we love than to a perfect stranger. Have you ever been in the middle of a heated discussion when the telephone rings? Your angry mate turns to answer the phone.... Suddenly, Mount Vesuvius is all sweetness and light. What's going on? You begin to rethink your entire approach to conflict: Next time, maybe you should just *phone* it in.

Why is it harder to be polite to your soul mate than to a perfect stranger? The reason is twofold: We have no *expectations* of a stranger, and we have no *history*. Marriage is all about expectations—expectations about how our mate should behave and how our mate should respond to us when we don't. When our mate fails to meet our expectations, we are disappointed, or disillusioned, or just plain angry. Every marriage has a history of disappointments, and it's within this history that every new conflict takes place. When a guest forgets his umbrella, it's the first time he's done it; when your husband forgets his umbrella, it's a reminder of hundreds of things he's forgotten in the past.

The first step, then, is to be less of a historian and more of an ambassador—an ambassador of *goodwill*. Goodwill is the simple willingness to approach your mate with the same respect, kindness, and consideration that you would a stranger. It sounds so basic—and it is. It is as basic to conflict resolution as oxygen is to life. Without it, a disagreement will go nowhere— because we *want* it to go nowhere. There is no rule or principle or "tip from the experts" that can overcome a heart attitude committed to hurt rather than heal.

This step is simple, but it is not easy. It requires a level of honesty and self-awareness that we're sometimes incapable of, especially if we're bitter or resentful over a history of past offenses and unsuccessful attempts at repair. But the starting point of all conflict resolution is to ask yourself, "Am I willing to be decent, even generous about this? Am I willing to approach this with an attitude of goodwill?"

In some cases, the answer is, "Sure, *I'm* willing to be decent about this—but *he's* not." What do we do when one of us is the Ambassador of Goodwill, while the other is the Secretary of War?

The most important thing is what we should *not* do. When our attempt at decency is met with a volley of fire, our natural instinct is to return fire. "If you're not going to be nice about this, then neither am *I!*" But when we surrender to our natural instinct, the argument quickly descends to the level of the lowest common denominator. Whoever is the smaller or meaner sets the tone for the entire conflict.

Instead of pulling each other down to a level of nastiness where no resolution is possible, the goal is for one of us to pull the other one up by *doggedly extending goodwill, even when goodwill is not offered in return.* In all interactions between you and your mate, there are three possible responses. A *natural* response returns evil for evil; a *satanic* response returns evil for good; but a *godly* response returns good for evil. This is what the Bible refers to as "returning a blessing for a curse." "While being reviled," Peter writes, "[Jesus] did not revile in return; while suffering, He uttered no threats, but kept entrusting Himself to Him who judges righteously" (1 Peter 2:23).

This kind of one-sided effort may sound self-sacrificing—some would say suicidal—but the truth is, the results of a one-person effort can be significant. Susan Page is the author of *How One of You Can Bring the Two of You Together.* She writes:

> The reason one person acting alone can make a major impact is that a relationship between two people is a single unit with two parts. When one person acts, the other is affected. Your behaviors and attitudes have an impact on your spouse. . . .

A marriage is like a seesaw. Even when one partner acts alone, it affects the other.

When you make a change in your behavior or your attitude entirely on your own, you can work a miracle in your marriage.[2]

No one should have to be the sole practitioner of goodwill in a marriage, but in reality, that's often the case. When conflict occurs, one of us is often angrier, or colder, or less willing to work things out than the other. That's when a "goodwill offering" is most important. Do you really want to resolve this conflict? Then refuse to wallow in the mud with your grumpy partner, and instead display an attitude of respect, consideration, and kindness.

Step 2: You Can Run, But You Can't Hide

Our first essential step began by asking the question, "Do you really want to resolve this conflict?" The second step poses a similar question—and it directs the question especially to men. The question is, "Is it more important to you to *resolve* this conflict or simply to *avoid* it?"

Research shows that in more than 80 percent of cases, men are the ones who attempt to avoid an approaching conflict. To put it another way, when it comes to the "fight or flight" reflex, husbands have a definite preference for flight. As one of the respondents to our survey asked, "Why does my husband consider discussing problems worse than torture?"

Several reasons have been suggested why this is true. Some studies have shown that men take longer than women to recover from the physical stresses of conflict. Their blood pressure stays elevated for a longer period, and their pulse takes longer to return to normal. Avoiding conflict, some say, is a self-preservation instinct for men. The motto here is, "He who fights and runs away will live to fight another day." Just imagine the benefits of refusing to fight *at all*.

Others, like linguist Deborah Tannen of Georgetown University, find the source of men's evasiveness in the different ways in which men and women engage the world itself. Men, she says, instinctively see the world in terms of *status*. Life for men is "a contest, a struggle to preserve independence and avoid failure."[3] But women instinctively view the world in terms of *connection*. Life for a woman is "a community, a struggle to preserve intimacy and avoid isolation."[4]

In Tannen's view, men and women live at cross-purposes, and our fundamentally different views of life lead to altogether different attitudes toward conflict. To a woman, who sees conflict in terms of *connection*, a disagreement may take a huge emotional toll, but she is willing to pay that price in order to "preserve intimacy and avoid isolation." But to a man, who instead sees conflict in terms of *status*, a disagreement may be interpreted as a challenge to his independence or as an accusation of failure. After all, if we're not getting along, doesn't that mean I've *failed?*

Whatever the cause, the fact remains that men tend to avoid conflict whenever possible—a fact that women do not need a scientific study to verify. Wives notice when their husbands refuse to engage, and it only makes matters worse.

Avoiding Conflict

Are you an avoider when it comes to conflict? Before you answer, remember two things: First, although avoidance is *typical* of men, it is not *limited* to men. Women are also avoiders at times, so don't discount the question on the basis of gender alone. Second, remember that avoidance takes many different forms. On our survey we asked the question, "Do you feel that you really *resolve* your conflicts most of the time? If not, what do you think keeps you from resolving them to your satisfaction?" Listen to some of the responses we received:

- *I rant and he puts up walls.*

- *No response at all from my mate one way or the other. Not rude, not mean, not disrespectful—just no response.*

178

- *I freeze up and stop communicating, so my wife just stops.*

- *Just yelling and not saying much.*

- *Always walking away.*

- *We tend to sweep the conflict under the rug after we sugarcoat it.*

- *We just stop fighting—rarely does the problem get solved. We want to end the fight, so we "apologize" and move on.*

These responses suggest at least three different means to the same end—avoiding a conflict at all costs. One respondent to our survey wrote, "I quickly apologize, whether I mean it or not, to make her stop yelling at me." This woman's approach is known as *escalation.* There is an entire range of escalation techniques that range from the annoying to the life-threatening: sarcasm, insult, contempt, shouting, rage, even physical violence. The goal of escalation is to raise the level of unpleasantness until the initiator simply backs down. Escalation says, "If you start something, believe me, I will finish it."

Another form of avoidance is the *quick fix,* in which one party suggests a solution—*any* solution—that will slap on a bandage and put an end to the conflict as quickly as possible. Unlike escalators, practitioners of the quick fix are willing to talk, but they're unwilling to deal with the *complexities* of an argument. Quick fixers often see themselves as efficient, or pragmatic, or action oriented—but their mates view them instead as uncaring or impatient. The quick fixer nobly says, "Let's put this behind us—just as fast as we possibly can."

A third form of conflict avoidance is known as *stonewalling.* Stonewalling is exactly what it sounds like—throwing up a thick defensive barricade and then huddling safely and silently behind it. Stonewallers are masters of nonverbal communication. They may shift their body away from the person talking, or avoid eye contact, or stare off into space, or simply get up and walk out of the room—anything to get the point across that "I don't want to talk about this." Trying to talk to a stone-waller is like trying to talk to a—you guessed it. Stonewalling says, "You can say whatever you want, but leave me out of it."

There are other forms of conflict avoidance as well, but all have a common goal: to simply *end* a conflict rather than do the difficult and sometimes messy work of resolving it.

A Costly Peace

To be honest, there is a reward for avoiding conflict: peace. But peace always comes at a price. Rebecca Cutter, the author of *When Opposites Attract,* says, "When couples who report that they 'never argue' are interviewed separately, one partner frequently admits that he or she has developed a pattern of 'peace at any price' and the price is usually the loss of self."[5] To put it another way, the price of peace is the loss of *dreams.* Avoiding conflict is sometimes nothing more than refusing to discuss what matters most to you. You may get silence or peace, but you will lose intimacy and oneness.

And there is another price for peace. After several years of marriage, couples learn which topics are most likely to generate a conflict, and avoiders simply refuse to go there. They begin to "rope off" large sections of the marriage and circumvent them as carefully as if they were minefields. But as one expert on minefields reminds us, "Land mines do not only kill and maim, they terrorize and trap entire communities." In Angola, entire villages have been cleared simply by planting land mines between the village and the nearest source of water. No one was injured; the mere *threat* of injury was enough to drive people away. Minefields not only kill; they *paralyze*—they keep us from going where we otherwise long to go.

How well can you get to know a country where vast sections of land are roped off and unavailable for access? How well can you get to know a spouse who has roped off topic after topic and posted "Danger: Risk of Personal Injury" signs? How intimate can you become when there is a risk of detonation with any casual misstep? How do you relax in a minefield? That's why Rebecca Cutter writes, "In relationships with a lot of avoidance, there is an air of tension and an absence of spontaneity, lending a lifeless quality to the communication."[6]

As the title of this step indicates, you *can* run from conflict —but you can't hide. If the price of peace is our dreams and our intimacy, then conflict avoidance is peace at too great a price.

But is it *always* wrong to avoid a conflict? Do we have to argue about every little thing? Isn't it best sometimes to just let it go? After all, Proverbs tells us that "a man's wisdom gives him patience; it is to his glory to overlook an offense" (19:11 NIV). Yes, sometimes it *is* best to let it go. But how do you decide when to let it go and when to confront? The answer is simple: Let it go when you *can* let it go.

If you decide to overlook an offense, but discover that your anger or resentment toward your mate is slowly growing, then you haven't let it go at all. If you keep score of the offense, waiting to bring it up at a later time, then you're still holding on to it dearly. If you tell yourself it's no big deal, but later find it hard to be warm and intimate with your mate, then maybe it was a bigger deal than you thought. Let it go when you *can* let it go, and when you can't, confront.

Only a sick person truly *enjoys* conflict—but a critical element of our marital backswing is the refusal to avoid conflict just for the temporary truce avoidance may provide.

Step 3: Identify Your Part in the Problem

Tim once came in from working in the yard and complained that something was irritating his right eye. He rubbed it, flushed it with water, and applied some saline drops, all to no avail. Finally, we called a friend up the street who is an ophthalmologist. Greg took a Q-Tip, placed it against the top of Tim's eyelid, and flipped the eyelid inside out. There, tucked back in the farthest crease of the inner eyelid, was a sliver of bark mulch no bigger than a gnat. Tim felt a little sheepish. What a fuss over such a little speck! "Actually, it's a good thing you called me," Greg said. "Bark mulch is a common source of a bacteria that can destroy an eye and cause blindness in less than twenty-four hours."

It's best not to judge a speck by size alone.

Jesus once said, "Why do you look at the speck that is in your brother's eye, but do not notice the log that is in your own eye? . . . You hypocrite, first take the log out of your own eye, and then you will see clearly to take out the speck that is in your brother's eye" (Luke 6:41, 42b). Without the aid of a mirror, it would be impossible to find a speck in your own eye. There is no way to turn the eye in on itself or to focus on anything so close. We look *past* the speck at the world around us, and the speck remains invisible—even if the speck is one that can cause serious harm.

On the other hand, it's a simple matter to spot a speck in someone else's eye. The other person's speck is well within our focal length, and it stands out in sharp contrast to the white of the eye around it. We're all experts at finding the speck in the other person's eye—and Jesus said that's the problem.

Three important lessons about conflict in marriage can be gleaned from Jesus' simple parable. First, *though I find it easy to recognize my mate's weaknesses, I find it almost impossible to identify my own.* Larry Crabb writes:

> Careful inspection of ourselves, particularly when we're angry, makes it clear that we suffer from a defect more severe than mere self-centeredness. The greatest obstacle to building truly good relationships is justified self-centeredness, a selfishness that, deep in our souls, feels entirely reasonable and therefore acceptable in light of how we've been treated.[7]

There is a natural astigmatism that infects all husbands and wives, and the disorder is passed unfailingly from generation to generation at the altar. It's a problem of focus; we all find it exceedingly difficult to identify what *we* contribute to a conflict. As Larry Crabb would say, *our* position always feels "entirely reasonable and therefore acceptable in light of how we've been treated." Jesus, in His parable, challenges this perspective and invites us to reconsider our "justified self-centeredness."

There is a temptation in any conflict to cast the entire blame on our partners, to cast ourselves in the role of hero and our spouses as the villain. But when we do this, we inevitably learn the wisdom of the saying, "Arguments wouldn't last very long if Truth were only on one side."

Tim: *When we built our house ten years ago, we asked the builder to leave off the deck. I wanted to build a better one, a much larger one, the kind you can only afford to do if you do it yourself.*

Joy: *It was four years before we had the time and the money to begin the project, and then it took four years to complete it.*

Tim: *I knew it would be a big project, and I wanted to be careful not to burden Joy with it. She had a lot on her plate already! I was very careful not to ask her to hold boards, or to hand up tools, or to help in any way.*

Joy: *Then one evening at dinner I began to comment about how long the job was taking, and how much trouble it was . . .*

Tim: *. . . and I went ballistic! I began to list point by point all the ways I had avoided asking for her help, and how I had done all the work, and how she had not been required to contribute anything. It was an iron-clad case. What could she say?*

Joy: *I said, "When you decide to take an entire Saturday to work on the deck, who do you think has to watch the kids all day and cover for the other responsibilities? And when you work right up until dinner time, and then head right back out to work some more, who do you think cleans up the dishes, helps the kids with their homework, and gets them ready for bed? Did you ever stop to think that when you decide how you're going to spend your time, you decide for me as well?"*

Tim: *And just like that, my ironclad case began to crumble. I hate it when that happens! I was so right and she was so wrong—that is, until I heard her side of the story.*

Joy: *Maybe that's why Proverbs 18:17 says, "The first to plead his case seems right, until another comes and examines him."*

In every case of speck-finding, we are looking past our own flaws and focusing on someone else's. Jesus instructs us to remember our own log. He is telling us to approach every conflict by first considering what part *we* play in it.

Family Systems therapists believe that problems not only originate *within* individuals, but in relationships *between* individuals. In other words, the problem isn't *you* and the problem isn't *me;* the problem is *us.* There is something in the way we relate to one another, something in the way our strengths and weaknesses collide, that causes this problem to exist at all. Couples in conflict commonly wonder, *Would I have this problem if I had married someone else?* Family Systems therapists would answer, "Maybe not. With a different partner, there would be a different *us.* With a different *us,* you would have different problems—*but you would still have problems.*"

He values order, but she values spontaneity. Nothing is wrong with either perspective, but when they come together in marriage, friction will result. Each may blame the other for the entire problem, but the truth is that some part of the problem belongs to each. And that brings us to the second lesson to be learned from Jesus' parable: *The bigger part of the problem belongs to me.*

Why would Jesus make such a blanket statement? Surely in at least *some* cases your mate is to blame. Surely there are times when the lion's share of the responsibility is the other person's. Why is it always *your* fault?

Jesus didn't say it's always your fault. He said that to keep a healthy and conciliatory perspective, we should always try to think of *his* problem as a speck and *my* problem as a log.

There are some very powerful benefits to this disproportionate perspective. It forces us to approach conflict with *humility* —a quality that stands in stark contrast to an attitude of "justified self-centeredness." Our debt to God vastly outweighs any debt owed to us by another human being. Our log, their speck—*yet our log has been forgiven*. A deep awareness of our own forgiveness creates a genuine humility as we approach our mates. A forgiven person is a humble person, and no attitude is more productive when it comes to resolving conflict.

Another benefit of the "my log, your speck" perspective is that it encourages you to take responsibility for your own actions, and to change the things that you can actually change. The difference between a speck and a log is not only a difference of size; it's also a difference of *accessibility*. A speck can be microscopic, requiring special tools and great skill to remove. A log can be removed by anyone—just grab hold with both hands and heave.

Marital researchers agree that it does little good to mope around, cursing the differences between you and your mate, waiting for your other half to get with the program and change. Instead, we are encouraged to occupy ourselves with changing what we *can* change—ourselves! Susan Page writes:

> Here is the bad news: Your partner won't change. *Give up on that.* . . .
>
> But with regard to finding a solution to your problem, *it doesn't matter.* Maybe you are right that your spouse is causing

the problem. It makes no difference whose fault it is; you can still solve the problem.

How? By figuring out what role you play—and making a slight shift in it. . . .

You have no control over your partner. You have already discovered that. But you have enormous control over yourself, your response to your partner, and the initiatives you take with regard to your partner.[8]

Want your mate to change her attitude? You'll find that trying to force a change in your partner's personality is like trying to grasp a speck with tweezers. *Your* attitudes and actions, on the other hand, are right there within your grasp. Just grab hold of the log and heave.

The third lesson to be learned from Jesus' brief parable is that *my own weaknesses keep me from seeing my mate's weaknesses objectively.* Notice what Jesus said: "First take the log out of your own eye, and then you will see clearly to take out the speck that is in your brother's eye" (Luke 6:42). He did *not* say, "Who are you to be removing the speck from someone else's eye?" No, the problem is not in our desire to remove the speck; the problem is that we don't see clearly enough to do it properly. As we said in the last chapter, one of the chief purposes of marriage is to help reshape each of us into the people God intends us to be. That process sometimes involves friction, and disagreement, and a good deal of speck removal. But speck removal should not be attempted by the clumsy, or careless, or callous. Blind men have no business doing eye surgery.

Rebecca Cutter writes, "Each of us thinks we see things as they are, but we see things as we are conditioned to see them. None of us is as objective as we would like to think. *What* we see is highly related to *how* we see."[9]

If you think that the problem is all your mate's, and that you are nothing more than an innocent victim, then you're not yet ready to take the speck out of her eye. If you think that you are the hero in your marriage and your husband is the villain, then your "justified self-centeredness" is obscuring your vision. If you're not ready to consider *your* role in the problem, then you won't have the steady hand and gentle touch necessary to perform surgery on someone else's eye.

These three preliminary steps alone could revolutionize your entire approach to conflict. But there are two more steps that can add even more to your chances of success . . .

CHAPTER twelve

takinG tHe Next steps

The first three steps in approaching the Seven Conflicts are to become an ambassador of goodwill, to refuse to avoid conflict when it occurs, and to approach every disagreement by attempting to identify your own part in the problem. The fourth step is to ask who *else* might have a part in the problem . . .

Step 4: Who's in the Room with You?

We once spoke at a marriage conference attended by a number of engaged couples who were still debating whether to tie the knot. One young couple came up to us during a break.

"I have a problem," the woman said, nodding toward her fiancé. "I don't trust him."

"Why not?" we asked. "What's he doing wrong?"

"It's nothing that he's *doing*," she said as she shook her head. "He says he loves me, but I'm just not sure he does. When he says he'll call me, I don't believe he will. And when his job takes him out of town, I'm not sure he'll ever come back to me."

"I keep trying to reassure her," her fiancé said hopelessly, "but it just doesn't seem to do any good. How can I prove to her that she can trust me?"

It was obvious that they had a Loyalty issue—and it was

also obvious that more was going on than meets the eye. We began to talk about their backgrounds and their upbringing, and before long the fact emerged that when the young woman was just a little girl, her father had left the family abruptly and never returned. She was devastated, and the pain of that betrayal was a wound that had never healed.

"This is not about you," we said to the young man. "This is about men in general. Your fiancée isn't asking whether she can trust *you*; she's trying to decide whether she can trust *any man at all*."

We advised the couple not to proceed into marriage until they pursued this issue with a counselor. This was not simply a Loyalty conflict; it was an *amplified* Loyalty conflict. The young man could spend his entire marriage trying to demonstrate Faithfulness and Priority to a woman who was unable to believe it. They would be destined to repeat the Loyalty conflict over and over again without hope of resolution unless she came to terms with this issue herself. And as we told the young man, it wouldn't be his fault. Every time they began the Loyalty conflict, someone else would be in the room with them. She would be confronting not only him, but her own father as well.

Psychologist and corporate advisor Tom Barrett encourages his clients to consider the question, "Who's in the room with you?" The question asks you to evaluate whether anyone or anything in your past or present might play an *amplifying* role in your current conflicts. Is any external fear or pressure intensifying your desire for Security, Loyalty, Responsibility, Caring, Order, Openness, or Connection? When you begin an argument with your spouse, is anyone else in the room with you?

The question "Who's in the room with you?" doesn't always imply a negative influence. Sometimes the amplifier is a positive experience from the past, a powerful role model, or a cherished experience that you long to recapture. As you consider the question "Who's in the room with me?" we would encourage you to think of both the positive and the negative, and to consider several different categories.

Your Childhood

A friend of ours tells us that when he was a young boy, his family experienced constant financial pressures. He remembers waking up at night to hear his mother and father arguing over how they would make ends meet, and whether it would be necessary for his mother to take a job to help earn additional income. Our friend lived with the constant fear that his mother would have to leave the family, and in his mind it all boiled down to a single principle: If you save money you keep your mother, and if you spend money you lose your mother.

It's no surprise that as an adult our friend has an amplified desire for Security, and that desire is directly related to money. Whenever the issue of money comes up his instinctive response is, "Do we *have* to spend it? Couldn't the money be saved?" The issue of spending versus saving is a source of conflict for many couples, but it's a far more difficult argument when a childhood fear is always in the room with you.

Past Relationships

For remarrieds, past relationships are enormous amplifiers of issues. One of the Seven Conflicts may have been the chief cause of the breakdown of the past relationship, and that creates a heightened fear of the pattern repeating itself. A woman whose previous husband was abusive may have heightened desires for Security or Caring. A man whose prior wife was irresponsible and disorganized may have an intensified desire for Order or Responsibility.

If this is your first marriage, think through your past engagements or even dating relationships: a boyfriend who never listened, a fiancée who unexpectedly broke off the engagement without explanation, a girlfriend who spent time with you but never wanted to be with your friends . . . In each case, an especially negative *or positive* experience may still be in the room with you as you attempt to negotiate the conflicts of your marriage.

Mom and Dad

Mom and Dad loom large throughout our lives. Though we all eventually leave home, for some of us Mom and Dad never really leave the room. A father's criticism or a mother's approval can be powerful influences, sometimes continuing long after the life of the parent. Loyalty conflicts are sometimes amplified by positive influences from the past—when a wife gives greater priority to her father's opinions than to her husband's, or when a husband weighs his own wife's performance against that of his saintly mother.

Cultural Expectations

As we said before, marriage is all about expectations, and when our expectations aren't met, it's a source of anger and disappointment. Sometimes our expectations come from the culture around us—expectations about roles, or masculinity and femininity, or acceptable behavior, or the inner workings of marriage itself. At times we unconsciously measure our mate against some unspoken standard without even knowing precisely what the standard is or where it came from. When our partner fails to meet that standard, we're all the more convinced that he has fallen short. After all, he's *supposed* to be like *this*.

Our cultural expectations can be deeply held and are seldom questioned. During an argument, an unspoken standard can be an unwelcome guest in the room.

Your Occupation

Chuck Douglas was a police officer in Oklahoma City in 1995 when a terrorist's bomb destroyed the Alfred P. Murrah Federal Building, killing 168 people and wounding countless others. Chuck was part of the initial team that searched frantically through the wreckage for survivors—an event that he has difficulty talking about to this day. In the weeks that followed, as Chuck internalized the horror, he grew increasingly angry and sullen. Less than a year later he and his wife were on the verge of divorce. They were not alone; it's estimated that in the years following the Oklahoma City bombing, more than *80 percent* of the rescue workers divorced.

Sometimes it's difficult to leave your work at the office. It's hard enough to argue with a husband; it's even harder when your husband is an attorney who always seems to slip into a "cross examination" style of discussion. In a conflict, the habits of your profession may tend to amplify certain issues. We need to try to leave the attorney outside and only allow the husband to take part in the discussion.

Current Stresses and Fears

No argument takes place in a vacuum. It takes place in the surrounding environment of daily anxieties, concerns, and distractions. Current events can act as catalysts that temporarily intensify certain issues. News of a friend who unexpectedly leaves her husband for another man may intensify your desire for Loyalty. A self-centered and thoughtless teenager may accelerate your desire for Caring and Appreciation. Long hours at home with a toddler may create greater friction with an introverted spouse who only wants to sit at home and watch TV. Your answer to the question "Who's in the room with you?" may change from day to day, or even from moment to moment.

What do we do once we've recognized an intruder in the room with us? What steps do we take when we realize that someone or something is amplifying an issue in our marriage? There are three steps that can help to minimize the impact of an unwelcome guest.

The first step is to *identify the intruder.* Look back through the list of categories above. Do you recognize anyone or anything that has played a role in the conflicts you've had in the past? Give the intruder a name, and then talk directly about it with your mate. The problem with our intruders is that they hide in the shadows. Though they amplify and intensify *other* arguments, they themselves are rarely the subject of scrutiny. By talking directly about them, we begin to understand the power they have over us, and that allows us to be prepared for them when they appear again.

The second step is to *anticipate when the intruder will show up*. Once you understand who is in the room with you, you'll begin to realize that he only shows up for special occasions. Our friend who grew up with constant financial pressures has an amplified Security issue, but a very level-headed approach to other disagreements. When you understand the intruder and the topics he's most likely to influence, you'll be able to anticipate his next assault.

The final step is to *do your best to lock the door.* It sounds easy enough, but to be honest, it's a difficult and continual struggle. The intruder is in the room with you because *he has the key.* These influences can have significant power over us—but they *can* be resisted. An attorney can remind himself that his spouse is not on the witness stand, and he can catch himself when he begins to take on that adversarial tone. A woman whose adoration of her father is causing Loyalty conflicts can choose not to bring Dad into the discussion and to remind herself that her husband's gifts may be different from those of her father. And a friend with financial fears can learn to put those fears into perspective and to loosen the purse strings—if only a little at a time.

The fifth and final step in preparing for the Seven Conflicts is to attempt to eliminate some things that could be holding you back . . .

Step 5: Identify Your Dead Ends

From time to time our children have suddenly decided that they are going to have things *their* way. All kids have this ambition from time to time, and like all kids ours tried a variety of techniques to obtain their goal. They whined, they wailed, they demanded, and they threatened. We, of course, made sure that none of it worked, and the child always ended up disciplined or grounded or staring sour-faced into a corner. Whenever this situation occurred, we asked the child two questions. First we asked, "Did you get what you wanted?" The answer was painfully obvious. Our second question was always, "Then why don't you try a different way of asking for what you want?"

Think back to the last conflict you had in your marriage. Did you get what you wanted? Michele Weiner-Davis, in her book *Divorce Busting,* says there is a reason we often don't get what we want in conflict:

> Solving marital problems can be like freeing oneself from quicksand. The harder you try to make things better, the less things change, which leads to frustration and, frequently, the decision that the marriage is dead. But there is a good reason that marital problems stubbornly persist, especially in the face of intense problem-solving efforts. Problems in marriages are maintained and aggravated by the particular way that people go about solving them.[1]

We don't get what we want, Weiner-Davis says, because of the way we go about it. That's understandable; after all, who knows if a particular effort will work until you actually try it out? What's harder to understand, however, is why we seem to try the same things over and over again even when we *know* they don't work. These ill-fated efforts are what we call "dead ends." Why would anyone in his right mind do what he knows won't work? Why does anyone steer a car up a dead end?

195

When something troubling happens in a marriage, the spouse most bothered by the situation usually tries to fix it. If that particular strategy works, life goes on. If it doesn't work, the fixer typically escalates his or her efforts or does more of the same. Spouse A reasons, "Perhaps I haven't gotten my message across," and, rather than trying a totally different strategy, employs the same ineffective strategy with greater intensity. Unfortunately, more of the same behavior from Spouse A yields more of the same undesirable behavior from Spouse B. This more-of-the-same approach not only maintains the problem, it increases it. In other words, the attempted solution becomes the problem.[2]

In conflict, we do the same unsuccessful thing over and over again because it *ought* to work. When it doesn't, we're convinced that we haven't done it hard enough, or often enough, or *loud* enough. So we do it again and again, with increasing determination, until there's a kind of meltdown. The "solution" has become the problem.

Tim: *In the evenings, when we want to relax, Joy and I like to trade back rubs. My favorite spot is right where my neck joins my shoulders. I get a lot of tension there—I like to think it's because the muscles are so massive that they exert too much pressure.*

Joy: *I call him "Arnold."*

Tim: *I like it when she takes her thumbs and really digs in hard. That's what feels best to me.*

Joy: *For me, there's a spot between my shoulder blades—I call them my "chicken bones"—where I get really tight. I like it when Tim rubs up and down along my chicken bones, but not too hard.*

Tim: *So when I give Joy a back rub, I naturally grab her by the neck and dig in hard.*

Joy: *And I say, "That hurts. Please rub along my chicken bones."*

Tim: *So I do—for a couple of minutes. Then my hands unconsciously start to work their way up toward her neck, and my grip begins to increase . . .*

Joy: *I worry about you sometimes.*

Tim: *And Joy always insists on rubbing my chicken bones. I hate that.*

Joy: *We go through this almost every time we trade a back rub. We're both so aware of what feels good to us that we naturally assume that it must feel good to the other person too—even when we know it doesn't work.*

Tim: *Joy and I have said that we should get tattoos on our backs. Hers would say, "Beware of neck," and mine would say, "Keep off the chicken bones."*

Earlier in the book we asked you to evaluate where you stand in relation to the Seven Conflicts. Is Security a bigger issue for you or for your mate? Is the need for Loyalty a driving force in your life? Is the desire for Order a source of conflict in your marriage? The issues that are most important to you will suggest certain instinctive approaches to conflict—but if your mate doesn't share the same issue to the same extent, that approach just might backfire. If you love Order, then you may think the best way to resolve a conflict is to take out pencil and paper and define the problem, suggest solutions, and establish new objectives. That may drive your partner *nuts*. But because the approach seems so natural to you, so *obviously* effective, you may find yourself doing it over and over again—*even though it doesn't work.*

We encourage you to take the time to identify your dead ends. Ask yourself, "Does my mate really *like* it when I rub his chicken bones? When I do that, do I get what I want?" After years of trial and error, what have you discovered *doesn't* work in your approach to conflict? Again, we encourage you to think in different categories . . .

Dead-End Times

For years we made the mistake of trying to begin a weighty conversation just before bedtime. After all, what other time is there? The kids are finally down, our work has momentarily ceased, and for the first time all day we are *alone*—so let's talk. It sounds reasonable; unfortunately, it was a dead end for us. One man complained on our survey, "Sometimes she drops a bomb on me just before I have to leave for work. There is no time then to deal with it, plus it preoccupies my thoughts and work performance." What about you? Have you tried to have a serious talk first thing in the morning? Proverbs 27:14 (NIV) says, "If a man loudly blesses his neighbor early in the morning, it will be taken as a curse." What about while you're trying to get dinner ready, or when the ball game is on? Are there times of the day that just don't work for one of you?

Dead-End Settings

You're at a restaurant, and there's something you need to discuss. Because you value Caring, you place a high value on taking the *initiative*. The best way to handle this, the most Caring thing to do, is to talk about this as soon as possible. But your mate doesn't seem to respond at all—because *his* issue is Obligation. You're in a restaurant, for crying out loud! What if someone overhears? What will people think? What are the places that you've found that just don't seem conducive to good discussion?

Dead-End Approaches

John Gottman claims that in 96 percent of cases you can predict the outcome of an argument after just three minutes.[3] How can you tell? The deciding factor is in the participants' basic approach. There is an old saying regarding actors: "By their entrances and their exits you shall know them." The same is true in the drama of marital conflict; our entrance sets the tone of the entire argument that follows, and so our entrance and exit tend to be very similar. If we begin with sarcasm and contempt, we will end with sarcasm and contempt. If we begin by shouting, we will end by shouting.

What are your first words when you want to bring up an issue? If you've told yourself, "I *have* to raise my voice; it's the only way she'll listen," then you may have doomed the discussion before it even starts.

Dead-End Words

Authors Sybil Evans and Sherry Cohen describe the problem of "hot buttons," words and phrases that generate such an emotional reaction from one's mate that they can stop a discussion cold.[4] In marriage we all learn each other's hot buttons, and in a really angry exchange we sometimes play each other like an accordion. One woman had this to say on our survey: "I wish he would not say the word 'clearly.' This drives me insane! He might as well say, 'It's not rocket science, Abbie.'"

Here's a partial list of hot buttons we've hit or heard of:

Don't be childish
That's not fair
Let's be logical about this
Be reasonable
You started this
You're just like your mom/dad
You're being defensive
Don't be so sensitive

We don't always push our mates' buttons on purpose. Sometimes in the heat of battle we use an unfortunate word or phrase quite by accident, but our mates will still naturally assume our intent. If you didn't mean it, then why did you *say* it? "When there are many words, transgression is unavoidable," Proverbs 10:19 warns us—or as another man put it, "Sometimes I talk so fast that I say something I haven't thought of yet." The best time to remove a few words and phrases from your vocabulary is *before* a conflict begins.

Dead-End Strategies

All of us have prize-winning "techniques" that we've developed to help make our point—and sometimes those techniques are nothing but dead ends. On our survey we posed the question, "If you could change one thing about the way your mate argues, what would it be?" Consider a few of our respondents' complaints about their partners' bad strategies:

- *He tries too hard to say what he thinks I want him to say.*

- *I wish she would not compare me to her former husband.*

- *Why does he have to come up with an illustration for everything?*

- *She takes a small criticism and blows it up by saying, "Oh, yes, I'm the biggest, stupidest woman in the world . . ."*

- *Sometimes I have a hard time figuring out what I really want to say, and he interrupts because he thinks he has figured it out for me.*

- *He is computer literate and too smart for his own good. He calculates and categorizes everything, and this frustrates me.*

- *I wish she would slow down the torrent of words.*

There is a story told about Thomas Edison, the inventor of the incandescent light. He experimented with thousands of substances before finally coming up with a suitable material for the filament, a simple piece of paper coated with carbon. Once, in the midst of the thousands of unsuccessful trials, he told a friend about his endless dead ends. "Then you haven't learned a thing," his friend lamented. "Of course I have," Edison corrected. "I've learned thousands of things that don't work."

Knowing what *doesn't* work between you and your mate is a major head start. By taking the time to identify your dead ends, you clear the way for more positive approaches that can truly make a difference in conflict. Are you getting what you want out of your marital discussions? If not, then maybe it's time to try a different way of getting what you want. In the next chapter we'll introduce you to one of those positive approaches, a technique we call "Moving Toward the Fence."

Before we leave this chapter, we want to reemphasize the importance of the "backswing." Americans tend to be very pragmatic people with a strong preference for action over mere reflection. Never mind all the discussion; just tell me what to *do*. We need to remember what Paul told us in his epistle to the Romans—we are transformed by the renewing of our *minds*. We have a stubborn habit of trying to change our experience simply by altering our behavior. We try to change from the *outside in*. Paul reminds us that the only way we can significantly alter our behavior is from the *inside out*—by changing the way we think.

Bobby Clampett finds that even professional golfers tend to ignore the backswing. Can you blame them? After all, the swing is where the action is; the swing is what makes the ball go. But Clampett likes to remind his colleagues that the real action is over before the swing even begins. Concentrate on the backswing and everything else is just follow-through.

You may feel a temptation to gloss over these introductory steps and to skip ahead to the practical "how tos" in the chapters ahead. We want to encourage you to resist this temptation and to carefully reconsider the concepts in the last two chapters. *This is the backswing of conflict resolution.* If you put in the practice time here—if you work to become an ambassador of goodwill, determine not to run from conflict, seek to identify your part in every problem, search for outside influences that might be amplifying your disagreements, and identify your dead ends—then the practical principles in the following pages will be a natural follow-through for you. But if you ignore these concepts, if you shortchange your practice time and hurry off to the first tee, you may find that you've already made errors that will be difficult to correct once a conflict is under way.

quick take

For Chapters 11 and 12

If you want to improve the style of conflict between you and your mate, there are five preliminary steps that can make all the difference.

Step 1. Become an ambassador of goodwill. Goodwill is the willingness to approach your mate with the same respect, kindness, and consideration that you would a stranger. It sounds simple, but the fact is we're often more polite to perfect strangers than we are to our own partners. That's because we often have bitterness and resentment over past conflicts, and that leads us to communicate with sarcasm, criticism, blame, and contempt—and we get nowhere with that approach. What do you do if you present a "goodwill offering" and your mate turns a cold shoulder? That's when it's *most* important to maintain goodwill. Instead of wallowing in the mud with your grumpy partner, your good attitude will encourage your mate to improve his.

Step 2. You can run, but you can't hide. Some people would rather avoid conflict altogether, and in more than 80 percent of cases it's men. Men commonly try to avoid conflict in one of three ways. *Escalation* threatens to raise the level of unpleasantness until the initiator backs down. The *quick fix* is an attempt to slap on a bandage and put an end to the conflict as quickly as possible. *Stonewalling* is avoiding conflict altogether by turning away, avoiding eye contact, or simply walking out. It's all right to overlook an offense when you really *can* overlook it—when you don't dwell on it or allow it to drive a wedge between you and your mate. Otherwise, it's best to confront the issue. The short-term reward for avoiding conflict is peace, but it's peace at too great a price—the price of intimacy.

Step 3. Identify your part in the problem. Jesus told us to remove the log from our own eye before we attempt to remove the speck from someone else's. Three important lessons come from Jesus' words: First, *though I find it easy to recognize my mate's weaknesses, I find it almost impossible to identify my own.* We often cast ourselves in the role of hero and think of our mate as the villain, but there's always *some* fault on *both* sides. The second lesson is that *the bigger part of the problem belongs to me.* This perspective allows us to approach our mate with an attitude of humility, and it keeps us focused on the things that we can really change. The third lesson is that *my own weaknesses keep me from seeing my mate's weaknesses objectively.* Speck removal is an important service—we just need to make sure we can see clearly before we attempt it.

Step 4. Who's in the room with you? This question asks you to consider whether anyone or anything in your past or present might be playing an *amplifying* role in your conflicts. The amplifier could be a negative experience you hope to avoid or a positive experience you wish to recapture. Think through your childhood, your past relationships, your mom and dad, cultural expectations, your occupation, and current stresses and fears. Once you identify an intruder in the room with you, try to identify the issues where it most often appears, and do your best to resist its influence. Conflicts are hard enough without being amplified!

Step 5. Identify your dead ends. We all have instinctive approaches to conflict—and some of them just don't work. Even when they don't, we have a tendency to repeat them again and again, which only makes the problem worse. What *doesn't* seem to work for you no matter how many times you try? Do you have dead-end times, settings, approaches, words, or strategies? We need to identify these habitual dead ends and eliminate them to make room for more productive approaches —which you can read about in the Quick Take at the end of the next chapter.

CHapter thirteen

moving toward the fence

Joy: Tim and I once had a disagreement about the kids. I felt especially burdened about something the kids were going through, and to me, Tim just didn't seem to care.

Tim: Caring has been a big issue for us in our marriage. Joy naturally seems to care about almost everything more than I do.

Joy: And that's been hard for me. It makes me feel like I have to carry the entire emotional burden of the family.

Tim: I tend to feel that she wouldn't have to carry such a burden if she would just not concern herself with so many things.

Joy: We've had this discussion many times over the years—it's one of our Seven Conflicts. Once, in a moment of complete frustration, I looked at Tim and said, "Why can't you just CARE more?!"

Tim: And I glared back at Joy and said, "Why can't you just WORRY less?!"

Joy: And then we just sat there staring at each other. It suddenly dawned on us that we were powerless to erase such a fundamental difference between us. Tim is never going to care as much as I do, and I cannot simply flip a switch and care less.

Tim: I'm not going to evolve into Joy, and Joy isn't going to

transform into me. We have to live together and love
each other as different kinds of people—and so do you.

Joy: *But this is the important thing: Even though Tim will*
never become just like me, he can become more like me.

Tim: *And the other way around.*

Joy: *What?*

Tim: *It's the other way around, too. You can become more*
like me.

Joy: *Whatever.*

The Fence Between Us

If you could choose one photograph to represent what marriage is really like, what would the photograph show? Judging by many of the book covers and movie posters we've seen, the photograph would show a happy couple wandering hand in hand through an open meadow. Not bad—but our photograph would look a little different. Don't misunderstand—there are many moments like that in marriage. Thank God for them! But to really represent the day-to-day reality of married life, we think the photograph would have to be slightly altered . . .

Picture a happy couple wandering hand in hand through a beautiful meadow. Now picture between them a wooden barrier; they are holding hands *across a fence.* At points the fence is so low that they are unaware it even exists between them. At other points the fence begins to rise until each partner in the couple is forced to break hands and walk alone. At some points the fence is almost invisible; at other points the fence becomes a solid wall, completely obscuring one partner's view of the other.

Each of us lives in a kind of "meadow." Your meadow is your field of dreams, your own collection of personal preferences, penchants, and predilections. You like this, but you don't like that. You want to live this way, but you do not care to live that way. Your meadow is your "home field," and each of us hopes to play the game of marriage on his own home field. Unfortunately, your mate occupies a very different meadow, and no one wants to give up the home field advantage.

When we marry, we assume that we're both building a house in the same meadow. But as the years go by, we discover that we're not—at least, not all the time. Much of the time we're only occupying adjacent properties. Our meadows do overlap, of course—we both love this, we both hate that—but over time our conflicts help us to understand that in many ways we each live in our own personal field of dreams.

We hold hands across a fence. That's a good picture of the process of a marriage. We hold on as tightly as we can, but when the fence rises to the point where we can no longer walk together, we release our grip and continue to follow the fence alone, looking for the next break in the wall where we can join hands once again.

Why don't we just knock down the fences and live together in one great big meadow? Why let a wall keep us apart? Or why doesn't one of us just jump the fence and join the other in *his* meadow?

If you think about it, that's exactly what you've tried to do over and over again. How many times have you said to yourself, *I'm tired of being the one who always:*

(a) *has to care about everything.*
(b) *has to clean up around here.*
(c) *cares about what other people think.*
(d) *has to think about the kids' safety.*
(e) *has to suggest getting together with other people.*
(f) (you fill in the blank)

Remember what happened next? In your frustration you made one of two choices: You either began to insist that your mate become much more like you (*you* start inviting people over), or you made the commitment to jump that fence once and for all and become just like your mate (I'm just going to *forget* other people). In other words, you either called to your mate to come and live in *your* meadow, or you tried to jump the fence and make yourself at home in *hers*.

How did it work?

If you're like most people, it did work. If you convinced your mate to join you in your meadow, there was a wonderful feeling of warmth and unity and teamwork—for a day or two. Then one day you began to notice your mate lingering near the fence, gazing longingly at her own meadow once again. A week later she was nowhere in sight. Where did she go?

Home.

Can you really blame her? If you were the one who made the commitment to amend your ways and become just like your mate, how long did it last for you? Why is it that, despite our best efforts and intentions, we always seem to wander home to our own field of dreams? Introverts remain introverts, those who Care continue to Care, and lovers of Order remain planned, prepared, and organized.

The reason we don't permanently jump those fences is that we can't. David Keirsey and Marilyn Bates, in their book *Please Understand Me: Character and Temperament Types*, begin their book with these words:

> The point of this book is that people are different from each other, and that no amount of getting after them is going to change them. . . . Of course, some change is possible, but it is a twisting and distortion of underlying form. Remove the fangs of a lion and behold a toothless lion, not a domestic cat. Our attempts to change spouse, offspring, or others can result in change, but the result is a scar and not a transformation.[1]

According to the authors, each of us has an underlying *form,* a basic temperament or personality type. Attempts to change that underlying form are doomed to failure. "People can't change form no matter how much and in what manner we require them to," they write. "Form is inherent, ingrained, indelible."[2] But how does this fit with our earlier assertion that one of the chief purposes of marriage is to help shape one another into the people we should be? If our basic form can't change, what *can?*

The Fence You Can't Jump

It may be true that each of us has an inherent, ingrained, indelible *form*—but surrounding that inner form is a lifetime of choices, behaviors, and preferences that *can* be changed. Every computer comes with a BIOS chip—an unchangeable, unprogrammable set of instructions that tells the computer what to do when the power is first turned on. But the computer also comes with software that can be added or removed, and it's the software that determines the computer's everyday look and feel. We may all have a God-installed BIOS chip, and although it may be hopeless to attempt to reprogram it, we are all loaded with software too. That's where change can occur, and those changes and adjustments are critical to our enjoyment of marriage.

How do you tell the BIOS chip from the software? How do you know when you're asking your mate to change a simple habit and when you're asking him to alter his original programming? That's what the Seven Conflicts are all about. The issues that you return to again and again may be helping you identify your basic form. The fence that you can't jump may be telling you what you can't change.

But if there are fundamental things we can't change about one another, are we doomed to live out our marriages in frustration, endlessly enduring all of our mate's annoying differences without any hope of improvement? If there are fences we just can't jump, then what *can* we do?

We can learn to *move toward the fence.*

Approaching the Fence

Though not every fence can be crossed, every fence can be *approached*. That's exactly what we're recommending—that couples explore the boundary between their unchangeable form and their changeable habits. Couples should change what they *can* change in the name of love, and when they can't jump the fence, they can still learn to move toward it. This concept of "moving toward the fence" is the crucial component in learning to live and love with the Seven Conflicts, and it consists of four major steps.

Step 1: Identify Your Home Field

In chapters 3 through 9 we described the seven fundamental issues that underlie most of the ongoing conflicts in marriage. At the end of each chapter we included a kind of inventory to help you identify where you and your mate stand in relation to that issue—to help you identify your *home fields*. Who is the more Security-oriented of the two of you? Who cares the most about Loyalty? Who feels the greater sense of Responsibility, and what is your natural style of Connection?

We also asked the question, "Who's in the room with you?" to encourage you to consider whether anyone or anything might be amplifying the effect of any of these issues. Do you come from a broken family? Have you been married before? Does your occupation lead you to interact in an adversarial style? Are there other current fears and anxieties that might be intensifying an issue for you?

As you review your answers to the Seven Conflicts inventories, do you recognize the familiar boundaries of you and your mate's home fields? Are you able to recall recurring arguments between you, and are you beginning to recognize the issues behind them? Most important of all, *are you beginning to anticipate the future conflicts that you and your mate are likely to have?*

Here's a critical point: You don't have to understand your

mate's home field in order to *identify* it. In fact, quite the opposite is true: The reason we have to do the hard work of recognizing another home field is precisely because we *don't* understand it. It's not our way of seeing things, and it's not our way of living. It just ain't *natural.* On our survey we asked the question, "What is the biggest thing you still don't understand about your mate?" Listen to some others who are struggling to identify home fields:

- *Why does he have to refer to how others do it before we can make a decision?*

- *Why is he unable to effectively deal with life's little stresses?*

- *Why does he hide himself in being busy instead of staying home?*

- *Why does he get so angry over inanimate objects (cars, tools, lawn mowers)?*

- *Why does she worry so much about things out of her control?*

- *Why is his mother so important to him?*

If at this point you think you're beginning to *recognize* what's important to your mate, but you still have no idea *why,* that's okay. You're still ready for the second step in moving toward the fence.

Step 2: Measure the Distance to the Fence

Every major league ballpark has numbers on its outfield walls: 360, 380, 425 . . . The numbers themselves have no effect on the game; it's not as though the batter can set his bat for "425." The numbers simply tell the batters how far they have to go to hit a home run. But sometimes it's very helpful just to know how far you have to go.

As you and your mate identify your home fields, take a

measurement. Who is farther from the fence? How extreme are you in relation to each of the Seven Conflicts? How far would you have to go to reach the fence? How much can you change?

Imagine a husband who is an extreme introvert, one who prefers to spend the majority of his time entirely in seclusion. He always comes home from his job exhausted, not only because of the job, but because of the demands of all the people he is forced to interact with each day. He opens the front door and heads directly for his den, where he turns off the lights, flops down on the La-Z-Boy, and turns on the television. His one desire for the evening is to be left *alone*.

Now imagine that his wife is a very moderate extrovert. She enjoys being around people, but she is also drained after too much interaction and enjoys a little time to herself. She likes to invite friends over to the house, but only a few, and only from time to time.

Who is farther from the fence?

As in baseball, the measurement itself doesn't affect the game—it just tells you how far you have to go. The husband in our illustration has to realize that his approach to people is more extreme than his wife's and that he will have to do some serious soul-searching about adjustments he can make. And his wife will have to remember that, even though her husband's starting position is more remote than hers, there are still changes she can make as well. She will probably find her changes easier to make; the farther from the fence you are, the more difficult the first steps feel. Sometimes our meadows are so remote that it's hard to spot the fence at all.

Measuring the distance to the fence is important because of a process that takes place in marriage known as *polarization*. Polarization is the tendency to alter your personality in response to your mate. It happens to everyone to some extent, and it happens in one of two ways.

Imagine a woman who is very Security-oriented. She thinks constantly about the safety and well-being of her children and spares no effort to make sure they are secure and provided for. Security is her *dream*. Now imagine that she marries a man who is similarly oriented. He helps her to realize her dream of Security, and so she feels the freedom to loosen her own grip on this dream of hers. After all, she can afford to; someone else is helping to make her dream come true. Because her mate is also Security-oriented, she becomes *less* Security-oriented herself.

But suppose she marries a man who is very differently oriented. He thinks that the kids can take care of themselves and that a little risk taking (or a lot of risk taking) is perfectly acceptable. It will teach them how to stand on their own two feet. In this scenario, the woman may become much *more* Security-oriented. She feels that she has no choice; since he doesn't care about Security, she has to care all the more.

Are there areas in your marriage where you feel that you and your mate have polarized? Has your mate's difference in perspective caused you to become even more desperate in pursuit of a dream? Is your husband so extroverted that you have compensated by withdrawing, so that you are now more introverted than you were as a single person? Is your wife so disorganized that your desire for Order now borders on the compulsive? Husbands and wives who have experienced polarization sometimes comment that they no longer recognize themselves. "I used to be so spontaneous," one might say. "But since I married Ryan . . ."

A wonderful benefit of moving toward the fence is that it reverses the effect of polarization. Once a husband recognizes that his wife is Security-oriented and that he is not, he can measure the distance to the fence—what changes can he make that will move him closer to his wife's meadow? As he begins to make those changes, small though they may be, his wife senses his movement toward her. She can see that he is becoming more conscious of the children's Security, and that allows her to become less. Each movement toward the fence is greeted by a reciprocal movement from the other side.

In our first step we encouraged you and your mate to try to identify your home fields—to determine where each of you stands in relation to the Seven Conflicts. Who is more Security-oriented? Who cares more about Responsibility? In the second step we asked you to identify where you stand in relation to each other. Just how far apart are you, and who is farther from the fence? Once you've measured the distance to the fence, it's time for the most important step of all . . .

Step 3: Move Toward the Fence

In the third step it's time to take action. Now that you know where you are and how far you have to go, it's time to ask, "What can I do to move closer to my mate's dream?"

To be honest, some people balk at this question. "Why should I change at all?" they ask. "It's her problem; she's the one who needs to change." In case this thought is crossing your mind right about now, allow us to remind you of two points we brought up earlier.

First, remember that the problem belongs to *both* of you. There is something in the way you relate to each other, something in the way your strengths and weaknesses collide, that causes this problem to exist. In the previous chapter we encouraged you to try to identify *your* part in the problem—or, as the Bible says, "Look for the log in your own eye." It may not be all your fault, but there's *something* you could change.

Second, remember that this process is not only about solving a disagreement, but becoming the person God intends you to be. In fact, the entire process of "moving toward the fence" could be expressed as "allowing God to shape you through the dreams and desires of your partner."

In King David's life there was an occasion when his own son rebelled against him and tried to seize the kingdom. Absalom came with an army seeking his father's life, and David barely had enough time to grab a few possessions and run for the back door, escorted only by his household and personal bodyguard. As he fled, a peasant named Shimei began to curse David and throw stones at him. "Get out," he shouted. "Get out, you man of blood, you scoundrel!" The head of David's bodyguard said to the king, "Let me go over and cut off his head." David's response is instructive: "If he is cursing because the LORD said to him, 'Curse David,' who can ask, 'Why do you do this?' . . . Leave him alone; let him curse, for the LORD has told him to" (2 Samuel 16:7, 9–11 NIV). What humility! David, the king of an entire nation, was willing to consider the possibility that God might actually have something to say to him through the mouth of a *peasant*. Is it unreasonable to consider that God might also have something to say to me through my *equal*? The humbling question we all need to ask ourselves is, "Am I willing to consider that God might be trying to say something to me through my mate?"

What would it really look like to move toward the fence? Let's consider a specific example. Let's imagine that a husband, reflecting on the Seven Conflicts, begins to understand that his wife is far more Security-conscious than he is, and that this difference has been the source of many disagreements between them. He decides to sit down and make a list. At the top he writes, "What are the things that my wife worries about most?" He begins to write: the kids, the finances, the house, our health, the economy, the schools, the past, the present, the future. . . . He stops. What *isn't* she worried about? He begins to feel that sense of despair, that feeling of being overwhelmed that he always feels when they try to discuss this issue. He feels like the man who wrote on our survey, "Her fears are STAGGERING." Where would he even begin? And what's the point? Even if he dealt with one issue of Security, another would be there to instantly take its place.

But this time he decides to ignore his discouragement and push forward. He starts a new list. "What is the *biggest* threat to my wife's Security *right now?*" He recalls that his wife heard a news report last month about several break-ins in their city. She has mentioned several times since that she fears *their* house might be broken into, especially while he's out of town. Each time he responded the same way: The break-ins were on the other side of town, this is a much safer neighborhood, our house is an unlikely target, and we can't afford an expensive alarm system right now. Of course, that did nothing at all to help her desire for Security.

He asks himself, "What *would* help her desire for Security? What can I do that would make her feel safer? How can I move toward the fence?" As he ponders, his mind begins to wander. *Why does she even* care *about these things? Why can't she just put them out of her mind?* He looks within himself and tries to drum up some fear of his own of burglary or assault. He can't. These fears make no sense to him at all.

But he shakes off these thoughts and reminds himself that he doesn't *have* to feel the same concerns about Security that she does. This is about *her* home field, not his. He goes back to his thinking, and finally an idea occurs to him.

He drives to Home Depot and buys three motion sensors, one for each exterior door of the house. They are easily wired into the light beside each door, and they instantly turn the light on if anyone comes within thirty feet of the door. Next, he stops at Radio Shack and buys a set of window stickers that say, "This House Protected by a Home Security Alarm System." He doesn't *buy* an alarm system—they can't afford that right now—he just buys the stickers. He remembers reading somewhere that the greatest value of an alarm system is its *deterrent* effect. The mere threat of an alarm system is enough to scare a lot of bad guys away.

He shows his wife his new additions to the house: a motion sensor at every exterior door and a warning sticker in the corner of every accessible window. He also tells her that he looked at prices for basic alarm systems. He didn't *buy* one, but he did consider prices.

And how does his wife respond to his ambitious first step toward the fence? She is grateful, but not as grateful as he expected. He was sort of hoping that when she observed his new-found interest in Security, her preoccupation with Protection and Provision might instantly begin to diminish. Because he was now more interested, she could be less interested . . . In no time at all the topic of Security would just disappear! To put it another way, when he took his first baby steps toward *her* meadow, he was sort of hoping that she might take a flying leap into *his*.

Sorry.

He momentarily forgot that Security is not just a notion for her; it's a *dream*. For too many years he has been oblivious to her concerns in this area, and in response she has become even *more* Security conscious—she has polarized. Far from satisfying her full desires for Security, his first step toward the fence only raised her hopes that more steps might be forthcoming. Now can we talk about the kids, and the finances, and the schools?

He feels another twinge of despair. Has he opened Pandora's Box? Has he created expectations that he knows he can never fulfill? But rather than give in to discouragement, he wisely decides to take the *long* view. He has taken a first step—a *good* first step—but he will have to take a second step, and another one after that, before his wife will believe that this is anything more than another quick fix.

More steps toward the fence? But how is he supposed to do that? How is he supposed to remember what he doesn't remember? How is he supposed to continue to think about things that never cross his mind? Because these new intentions aren't natural to him, he'll tend to forget them. Is there anything he can do to help himself stay on track?

Sure there is. He can *cheat*.

Every year in the Pacific Northwest, hundreds of thousands of salmon begin their spawning run from the saltwater of the Pacific Ocean up the freshwater rivers of Alaska and Washington. Some travel as far as two thousand miles, and it's upstream all the way. Sometimes the salmon come to a small waterfall, and the only way up is to leap the entire distance. It's easy enough if you're young and lean, but a lot of salmon just aren't up to it. Without help, their trip (and their life) would end right there.

Help comes in the form of a "salmon ladder," a man-made device that looks like a series of small pools rising one above another from the base of the falls to the crest. The salmon no longer have to leap the entire height of the falls; now they only need to leap the short distance from one pool to the next until they reach their goal. Ardent evolutionists might consider this "cheating." After all, isn't the waterfall a part of nature's weeding-out process? Only the strong can make the jump, so only the strong survive. Conservationists take a different view. By allowing the salmon to "cheat," they greatly increase the number of salmon that will survive to mate and reproduce upriver.

Our husband, who is trying to move toward the fence of his wife's concern with Security, can build himself a salmon ladder. He knows that since Security is not his issue, it would be easy for him to take these basic steps and then forget Security completely. He wants to keep moving toward the fence, but he's going to need help.

He takes two of the "Home Security System" stickers and places one on the dashboard of his car and the other by his computer at work. Now, when he sees those stickers each day, he's reminded to ask himself the same two questions he asked before: "What can I do that would make my wife feel safer? How can I keep moving toward the fence?"

Think of yourself as a salmon. It's not hard to do. If you've decided to make an effort to move toward the fence, you've begun an upstream swim, and chances are you can already feel the current pushing against you. Now you come to the first waterfall, and you remember those nature films with the hungry brown bears that stand gaping at you from the top. What can you do to increase your chances of survival?

You can make yourself a salmon ladder. Ask yourself, "Is there some way I can take this one step at a time? Is there anything that can help me remember to do what I've decided to do?"

Over the years many husbands and wives have described to us their own homemade salmon ladders. One man who wanted to work on the issue of Caring told us that he had difficulty remembering to buy his wife a greeting card on special occasions, though she told him many times that it was important to her—it told her that he *cared*. He always meant to, but in all the busyness and distractions of life, he usually seemed to forget. He always thought of it last minute, but by then it was too late. So he went to the Hallmark store and bought an assortment of cards for all occasions and kept them in a file at home. Now when he remembers last minute, he's ready to go.

One busy woman writes at the top of each page of her calendar, "three nights per week." That's her way of reminding herself that she wants to leave three evenings free each week to help her communicate Priority to her husband.

Another man writes himself notes and places them in prominent places on his desk. "Ask her how she FEELS," one of them says, reminding him of his goal to try to connect the way *she* connects. Now when his eyes sweep his desk he is constantly reminded to do something that does not naturally come to mind when he talks with his wife.

To some people, the suggestions above seem forced and artificial. A wife who wants her husband to be more Caring wants him to *think* about buying her a card; she doesn't want him to just mechanically pull one out of a jumbo file. That's not an expression of Caring; that's just efficiency. In fact, it feels like the exact opposite of Caring—the file method is something you do so you don't *have* to care. You don't even have to think. And what about the woman who writes "three nights per week" on her calendar? Some Priority! If she really *wants* to spend three nights per week with her husband, why does she need the reminder? The fact that she has to *make* herself alter her schedule shows that her husband is *not* a Priority. Why should these kinds of efforts encourage us at all? Because we're *all* like salmon.

The man with the jumbo file of greeting cards *does* care about his wife, but he's not very good at showing it. He forgets. When it comes to Caring, he's a salmon swimming upstream. The man whose desktop note reminds him to "Ask how she FEELS" actually does care how his wife feels, but his natural style of communicating is linear and factual, so he rarely communicates about feelings without *help*. In one way or another every one of us is a salmon fighting the current of his own inherent form, and every one of us has to jump the falls of busyness, forgetfulness, and distraction.

To be fair, the people who find these suggestions forced and artificial do have a point. The goal of a salmon ladder is to help the salmon keep moving upstream, not to give them a comfortable little pool in which to spend the rest of their lives. If the man with the jumbo file says, "I took care of the card thing; now I can get back to work," he has missed the point entirely. The next step for him is to stop simply signing the cards, "Love ya—Bob," and instead take the time to pen a meaningful message. Next, he might think about giving a thoughtfully worded card unexpectedly, for no reason at all. After that, he could begin to search for ways other than greeting cards to say, "I care about you." Each of these ideas is just another small pool higher up the ladder toward Bob's goal—to be a more Caring husband.

The jumbo file could be a move toward the fence or no movement whatsoever, all depending on Bob's *attitude*. At one of our conferences a man told us, "I bought these little red stickers, like the ones you use at garage sales. I told my wife, 'These stickers mean "I love you."' Then I stick them all over the house—on the mirror, on the telephone, anywhere she's sure to see them. Every time she sees one she thinks, *He loves me!* It takes no time at all, and it costs me less than a penny apiece."

That's one salmon that missed the falls.

These simple helps, contrived and artificial though they may seem at first, can be important. It's all right to cheat, as long as we remind ourselves what we're cheating *for,* and as long as we make it our goal to not have to cheat *forever.* We're temporarily using crutches, reminders, and cheat sheets to help us develop new habits—and habits quickly become a part of us. A writer named Frank Outlaw reminds us: "Watch your thoughts, they become words; watch your words, they become actions; watch your actions, they become habits; watch your habits, they become character; watch your character, for it becomes your destiny."

If something as simple as a new way of thinking can ultimately shape your destiny, then imagine what a new habit can do—a habit reinforced by incentives, reminders, and most of all encouragement.

That final word, *encouragement,* brings us to the fourth step in the process of moving toward the fence . . .

Step 4: Call to Your Mate Across the Fence

It would be difficult to overestimate the importance of encouragement for all of us. "But encourage one another daily," Hebrews 3:13 reminds us, "so that none of you may be hardened by sin's deceitfulness" (NIV). When we fail to encourage one another, we become open to deception, and a dangerous hardening effect can result. Without encouragement, situations that are merely troubling may suddenly seem hopeless; efforts that once seemed difficult may now appear impossible; improvements in our marriage that we were once willing to attempt no longer seem worth the effort. We've grown hard. We've lost *courage.*

The word *encourage* literally means "to impart courage to." We are *en-couraged* when someone gives us the courage, inspiration, and resolution to go on—a nutritional supplement that Hebrews tells us we all require on a daily basis. If encouragement is an essential nutrient for Christians in general, it's even more important between husbands and wives. There is a common deficiency of courage, inspiration, and resolution among marriage partners. The reason? On a day-to-day basis we forget to encourage one another.

Dennis Rainey, the founder and director of FamilyLife, gives this interesting piece of advice: "Catch your mate doing what's *right.*" Our eyes are naturally drawn to the error, the flaw, and the shortcoming in our spouses, and we're quick to point it out. We all catch our mates doing what's *wrong.* The good and the right somehow become the status quo; when things are going well, that's simply how it *should* be. Why bother pointing out the obvious? But when things go *wrong,* that's when we speak up. What a motivational environment! Our good efforts will go unnoticed, but our failures will all be posted in the Congressional Record. The result of this natural focus on the negative is a pervasive, toxic atmosphere of discouragement.

So your wife made dinner tonight. Are you supposed to say, "Thank you for doing exactly the same thing you've done every night for the last twenty years"? That's *exactly* what you should say, for the simple reason that she's made dinner every night for the last twenty years—without *encouragement.* Did you ever wonder what will give her the courage, inspiration, and resolution to make dinner *tomorrow?*

Maybe we can't encourage one another for every thankless chore, but we can do a lot better job than we're doing now. We can become much more aware of what our mates are doing *right,* and we can thank them and encourage them for their efforts—especially their efforts to move toward the fence.

As we said before, the problem is that every marriage has a history. When you decide to take that first tentative step toward the fence, how is your mate supposed to view it? Is it a preview of coming attractions, a first glimpse of a whole new you? Or is it just one more inconsequential effort in a long history of apathy and neglect? When an atmosphere of discouragement prevails in marriage, we sometimes paint a mental portrait of our mate surrounded by clouds and gloom. When we do this, even positive steps are viewed in light of our mate's history of failure.

This is an attitude that we have to consciously resist. When your mate makes the effort to move toward the fence, it's easy to say to yourself, *Why should this time be any different? It's never worked before.* We want to caution you that that attitude itself is *deadly.* A step toward the fence is a step of courage, and courage requires daily refueling. When your mate takes a step toward your world, you need to *call to your mate across the fence.*

If you see your mate take the slightest step toward your meadow, you need to call out, "Yes! That's right! That's exactly what I've been looking for! Please do more of that! Thank you for making the effort!" These words sound so strange, almost sarcastic—but that's only because we're so inexperienced at catching our mate doing what's *right.* One of the most common comments we hear from men is "I need to hear what I'm doing *right,* not just what I'm doing wrong."

Corporate coach and consultant Dan Sullivan has a helpful piece of advice for us here: "Evaluate progress in terms of how far you've come, not in terms of how far you still have to go." When we make the error of evaluating progress in terms of how far we still have to go, we doom ourselves to a constant state of discouragement. We constantly focus on what *wasn't* said, what *wasn't* done, and changes that *haven't* been made. The fact is, no matter how far we've come, we still have a long way to go. That's why we have to choose to shift our focus. As one man said on our survey, "The one thing I wish my wife understood about me is that I have come a long way."

If you live a mile from the fence, a single step forward seems almost useless—*but it's still a step forward.* That's one step away from the person you used to be and one step closer to your partner's dream. That's grounds for encouragement!

Call to your mate across the fence and see what begins to happen. Shout words of praise, encouragement, and affirmation. Work to create an atmosphere of courage, inspiration, and resolution, and you may find your mate is not only moving toward the fence, he's running.

For Chapter 13

each of us lives in a kind of "meadow." The meadow is our field of dreams, our own collection of personal desires and preferences. When we marry, we assume that we're both building a house in the same meadow. But as the years go by, we discover that we're not—at least, not all the time. Much of the time we're only occupying adjacent properties. We can't just knock down the fence between us, and we can't just jump the fence and join our partner in *his* meadow. What we *can* do is *move toward the fence*. This concept of "moving toward the fence" is the crucial component in learning to live and love with the Seven Conflicts, and it consists of four major steps.

Step 1: Identify your home field. Who is the more Security-oriented of the two of you? Who cares more about Loyalty? Who feels the greater sense of Responsibility, and what is your natural style of Connection? Are you beginning to recognize the familiar boundaries of you and your mate's home fields? Are you able to recall recurring arguments between you, and are you beginning to recognize the issues behind them? Most important of all, are you beginning to anticipate the future conflicts that you and your mate are likely to have? Remember: You don't have to *understand* your mate's home field in order to *identify* it.

Step 2: Measure the distance to the fence. As you and your mate identify your home fields, take a measurement. Who is farther from the fence? How extreme are you in relation to each of the Seven Conflicts? How far would you have to go to reach the fence? How much can you change?

Measuring the distance to the fence is important because of a process that takes place in marriage known as *polarization*.

Polarization is the tendency to alter your personality in response to your mate. If a Security-oriented woman marries a man who never thinks about Protection and Provision, the woman will become even *more* Security-conscious. She feels that she has no choice. Since he doesn't care about Security, she has to care all the more. Are there areas in your marriage where you feel that you and your mate have polarized? Has your mate's difference in perspective caused you to become even more desperate in pursuit of a dream?

Step 3: Move toward the fence. In the third step it's time to ask, "What can I do to move closer to my mate's dream?" Suppose a man begins to understand that his wife is far more Security-conscious than he is, and that this difference has been the source of many disagreements between them. He asks himself, "What is the biggest threat to my wife's Security right now?" He remembers that his wife has voiced concern about a possible break-in, so he buys three motion sensors, one for each exterior door of the house, and he places a warning sticker on each accessible window that says, "This House Protected by a Home Security Alarm System." He has taken a first step—a *good* first step—but there will have to be a second step, and another one after that, before his wife will believe that this is anything more than another quick fix.

But how is he supposed to remember to keep moving toward the fence of Security? Because these new intentions aren't natural to him, he'll tend to forget them. He wants to keep moving toward the fence, but he's going to need help—so he takes two of the "Home Security System" stickers and places one on the dashboard of his car and the other by his computer at work. Now, when he sees those stickers each day, he's reminded to ask himself the same two questions he asked before: "What can I do that would make my wife feel more secure?" His reminder system may seem forced and artificial, but it's for a good cause. He's temporarily using crutches, reminders, and cheat sheets to help him develop a new habit—the habit of thinking about Security.

Step 4: Call to your mate across the fence. There is a common deficiency of encouragement among marriage partners. Our eyes are naturally drawn to the errors, flaws, and shortcomings in our spouses, and we're quick to point them out. The good and the right somehow become the status quo. When things are going well, that's simply how it *should* be, but when things go *wrong,* that's when we speak up. The result of this natural focus on the negative is a pervasive, toxic atmosphere of discouragement.

We need to become much more aware of what our mates are doing *right,* and we need to thank them and encourage them for their efforts—especially their efforts to move toward the fence. When your mate takes a step toward your world, you need to *call to your mate across the fence.* If you see your mate take the slightest step toward your meadow, you need to call out, "Yes! That's right! That's exactly what I've been looking for! Please do more of that! Thank you for making the effort!" Call to your mate across the fence, and you may find that he moves toward your world even faster.

In the next chapter we explain how to "package" your words in a way that will win them the warmest possible reception. You can read about it in detail in chapter 14, or in the Quick Take that follows.

CHAPTER fourteen

speaking the truth in Love

Tim: *Joy loves to give gifts. Gifts for me, gifts for the kids, gifts for friends . . . I've told her that she married the wrong man—she should have been Mrs. Santa Claus.*

Joy: *I love to find the right gift for the right person at the right price.*

Tim: *And then she loves to wrap it the right way. Joy is a master gift wrapper—some of her packages are works of art. First she finds exactly the right paper. Even if it's your 42nd birthday, Joy will search until she finds wrapping paper that says, "So You're 42!"*

Joy: *I'm not that bad, but Tim would settle for paper that says, "Happy Bar Mitzvah." I think the paper should fit the occasion.*

Tim: *Next comes the wrapping itself. Joy wraps packages like an origami master. The seam is always on the bottom of the package, never on the top. A cut edge never shows. All the edges are crisp, the corners are tight. Joy wraps packages the way Marines make beds.*

Joy: *While Tim's packages look a little more like they were wrapped in old panty hose.*

Tim: *Then come the ribbons . . . not one ribbon, but half a dozen multicolored streamers all curled with the edge of scissors.*

Joy: I think the wrapping makes you appreciate the gift more. I think of the wrapping as part of the gift itself.

Tim: When we were first married, I didn't understand this. I looked at the wrapping as something that got in the way of the gift. I thought of wrapping paper the same way I thought of the foil on my cheeseburger—just rip it off and dive in.

Joy: A husband really is a work in progress.

Tim: Over the years, I've come to appreciate my wife's approach to packaging. Joy knows how to make almost anything look desirable. I really believe that she could make a brick look good. Not that she's ever actually given me a brick . . .

Joy: Not that I haven't thought about giving you one.

After one of our marriage conferences, a woman came up to us with a complaint about her husband. "We live in the city," she said. "My husband and I like to go walking together downtown. Sometimes when we're out for a walk an attractive woman will pass by. When that happens, my husband will stop and slowly look her over. Sometimes he'll even whistle, or make some comment like, 'Now there's a good-looking gal!' I hate it when he does that, and I tell him so—but whenever I complain he says, 'Look, that's just what comes to my mind when I see an attractive woman. I'm just telling you the truth about what I think. What do you want me to do, lie to you?'"

"What do you think?" she asked us. "Should my husband tell me the truth?"

"What do you *want* him to do?" we asked. She paused for a long moment.

"I want him to tell me the truth," she said slowly, "but not like *that*."

The woman's husband is an honest man. He's also a cruel and thoughtless man. Honesty is a wonderful quality, but *uncontrolled* honesty is like uncontrolled heat—it can injure and even destroy you. In the movie *Liar, Liar,* Jim Carrey plays an unscrupulous attorney who suddenly finds himself compelled to tell the truth, the whole truth, and nothing but the truth. He spends the rest of the movie being slapped, beaten, and humiliated by friend and foe alike. Just for being *honest?*

Honesty is an excellent virtue, but honesty alone can be brutal. Maybe that's why the Bible often recommends virtues in *pairs.* "For this very reason," Peter writes, "make every effort to supplement your faith with virtue, and virtue with knowledge, and knowledge with self-control, and self-control with steadfastness, and steadfastness with godliness, and godliness with brotherly affection, and brotherly affection with love" (2 Peter 1:5–7 ESV). The pursuit of moral virtue should be balanced by the intellectual pursuit of knowledge, and increasing knowledge needs to be tempered by self-control, and so on. One virtue is necessary to moderate and enhance another.

Was it wrong for the woman's husband to be honest? No, but it was wrong for him to be honest *only.* His honesty needed to be tempered by another virtue. As Paul expresses it in Ephesians 4:15, we need to speak the truth *in love.*

Wrapping Truth in Love

Think of your words as a kind of *product,* something you hope to sell to someone else. Most products begin their lives in the Engineering Department—that's where the original concept and design are developed. But once the original design is complete, the product leaves Engineering and goes to Marketing. That's where decisions are made about how the product should be *packaged.*

No successful product jumps directly from the Engineering Department to the retail shelf. Imagine breakfast cereals in brown paper sacks, or perfume sold in a jelly jar. Impossible! For some products, such as cosmetics and perfumes, more money is spent on the package than on the product it contains.

The product spends more time in Marketing than it does in Engineering.

Why? Because books are always judged by their covers, and perfumes are sold by the sensuous curves of their bottles, and panty hose are sold because their package is shaped like an egg instead of like everyone else's boring box. When it comes to the success of a product, packaging is almost *everything.*

But strangely, when it comes to marital communication, packaging is often ignored. If you think of your words as a product, that product should begin its life in Engineering; that's where you think of the idea you'd like to get across. But once that idea leaves Engineering, it ought to head directly to Marketing—that's where the idea is given its *look* and *feel.*

Paul encourages us to speak the truth in love. In communicating with our partners, truth should supply the *content,* and love should supply the *package.* All of us need to become packaging experts because in communication, as in manufacturing, packaging is everything.

In the movie *Ghost,* Sam and Molly are a young New York couple in love. Each time Molly tells Sam that she loves him, he replies by saying, "Ditto." What's wrong with that? The word *ditto* means "the same as stated above or before." Isn't that the same as saying, "I love you too"? Molly didn't think so. The *content* was the same—but not the *package.*

On our survey we asked the question, "If you could change one thing about the way your mate argues, what would it be?" One woman responded, "I'd change his matter-of-fact way of dealing with conflict. 'Here's the problem—Here's the solution—I'm sorry—Forgive me—Move on—NOW! Don't drag it out.'"

"I'm sorry—Forgive me"—aren't those the exact words most of us would like to hear in a conflict? What is this woman complaining about? Certainly not the content; this is a complaint about packaging. In fact, we received many complaints on our survey about a partner's lack of packaging skill. Here are just a few:

- *I turn off my ability to resolve when he sounds condescending.*

- *Even though she is not yelling, her tone of voice is sometimes saying, "How stupid can you be?"*

- *His body language is too loud and his words are too few, so I can only assume what he wants to communicate.*

- *Criticizing just makes the argument escalate into areas we don't even need to argue over.*

Packaging design is not a spiritual gift; it's an acquired skill. Like all skills, it requires focus and discipline and repetition to master. And like all skills, it can be improved by observing others who do it well.

A poet once wrote to his one true love, "Let me take you out into my garden, I want my roses to see you." That's a packaging expert's way of saying, "You don't look half bad today."

When Woodrow Wilson was president, he had a difficult time remembering names. He made a practice of saying, "I'm sorry, I've forgotten your name." If the listener responded with his first name, Wilson would say, "Oh no, I remember your first name as well as my own—it's your *last* name I can't remember." If the listener offered his surname Wilson would just reverse the tactic: "Of course I know your last name! It's just your *first* name that eludes me. . . ." Why did Wilson bother with this little ploy? After all, he was *president*. All he really needed to say was, "I meet a lot of people. Who are you again?" But Wilson understood something about the value of packaging, and his thoughtful bit of subterfuge allowed a lot of forgotten visitors to save face.

How strange that Woodrow Wilson would think to extend that kind of thoughtfulness to a stranger, and yet we often forget to do the same with those we love most. Speaking the truth in love is a *choice*. It takes time, and mental effort, and a spirit of goodwill—but the results are clearly worthwhile. If you're in doubt about this, just compare a few products *before* and *after* the packaging process.

The truth alone:	Who made that dress, Omar the Tent-maker?
The truth in love:	That's not my favorite of your dresses. I like your green one because it shows off your figure better.
The truth alone:	What happened to your hair?
The truth in love:	I see you had your hair done. Very stylish! Come here and let me take a better look at it . . .
The truth alone:	You look like you slept on gravel. You could pack a sandwich in those bags under your eyes.
The truth in love:	How did you sleep last night? I know you've had a lot going on lately. You know, you really deserve a vacation.
The truth alone:	You look like you've gained ten pounds.
The truth in love:	Nice day, isn't it?

Okay, some products may be impossible to package. But in most cases, it doesn't take much imagination to see the benefits of speaking the truth in love. Yet we often ignore this critical phase of the manufacturing process, and then when our message fails to win the respect and appreciation we hope for, we can't imagine what went wrong. Maybe the problem wasn't with the message at all; maybe it just needed a better package.

A Short Course in Packaging

Some spouses balk at the whole idea of "packaging" their thoughts. "Why should I bother?" they ask. "My mate is an adult. She can handle the truth. Why should I have to sugar-coat everything?"

We don't have to sugarcoat everything—only the things that are otherwise difficult to swallow. Vitamins are sugar-coated; so are most prescription drugs. A sugarcoating is only needed to make the bitter pill palatable—or as Mary Poppins would say, "A spoonful of sugar helps the medicine go down." When it comes to the Seven Conflicts, we're often discussing our deepest dreams and fears. Those are some powerful medicines, and a little sugar can help *a lot*.

And as for being able to handle the truth—yes, we can "handle" it, but what exactly does that mean? If it means we can bear to hear the words without cracking, of course we can. But if it means being able to give the words their warmest possible reception, then the fact is that truth alone seldom earns that kind of response. To those who insist on communi-cating the truth and nothing but the truth, we'd like to ask, "Do you get what you want?" If your mate has to constantly "handle" the naked truth, chances are *you* have to handle a lot of anger, coldness, and silence in return.

There is a rule of thumb that says it takes five positive re-inforcements to overcome the impact of one negative statement. Imagine if your finances worked that way. What would happen if every day you purchased one item that cost five times more than your entire day's salary? You would soon be bankrupt, of course. We find that many couples survive in a state of emo-tional bankruptcy due largely to the impact of poor packaging.

Couples often try to correct their deficit spending simply by increasing the number of positive statements they make each day. But do the math: the "five-to-one rule" reminds us of the inordinate power negative statements possess. Even if you decide to make five more positive comments to your mate each day, your entire day's effort can be neutralized by the impact of a single negative statement.

Everyone's marriage could benefit from more admiration,

gratitude, and praise, but the problem we're addressing here isn't the lack of positive reinforcement. The problem is failing to understand the relative impact of our negative statements. Instead of counting on praise and affirmation to compensate for our negativity, think instead of the advantage of learning to *repackage our negative statements in positive terms.* That's what speaking the truth in love is all about.

On our survey we asked, "Do you think your disagreements escalate more because of the way you argue or the topic you're discussing?" The majority of our respondents said that the real problem is the *way* they argue. Their disagreements are more about style than substance. This finding reinforces what we have long believed to be true: In a conflict, you only fight about a topic for the first three minutes. After that, you're fighting about the way you fight.

Our principle of *moving toward the fence* is nothing short of an invitation to couples to reenter some minefields—to revisit some issues that have been ongoing points of disagreement in the past. But no one should enter a minefield by stomping carelessly about. That only invites another explosion. Soldiers whose job it is to clear minefields crawl forward on their bellies, carefully probing the soil as they go. We need to exercise similar caution if we plan to revisit the site of earlier blasts. That's why the principle of *speaking the truth in love* is so crucial to dealing with the Seven Conflicts. We need to move toward the fence not only in substance, but in style.

That's where packaging comes in. Since speaking the truth in love is a skill, we can all learn to do it better. Let's pay a visit to the Marketing Department to see what we can learn about packaging design. Here are five simple principles to help us become better packagers of the cold, hard truth.

Principle 1: Choose a Package Your Mate Will Like

There is an old saying: "Diplomacy is to do and say the nastiest thing in the nicest way." Bringing up a complaint or a concern is sometimes a nasty business, so the goal is to look for the most diplomatic way to do it. Here are some helpful packaging tips your mate is sure to appreciate:

Introduce a Complaint with a Praise

"I need words of praise and reassurance often to feel valued," one woman wrote on our survey. "Words mean more than touch most of the time." Praise means a lot to all of us, though we often forget to give it. In marriage, we all need a regular reminder that we're not doing as badly as we think. Try introducing your next message with words like these:

"You are such a great mom/dad/wife/husband . . ."
"You are especially good at . . ."
"Thank you so much for . . ."

Express Approval Before Disapproval

This is much more than a childish desire for a pat on the head. As the philosopher Eric Hoffer put it, "No matter what our achievements might be, we think well of ourselves only in rare moments. We need people to bear witness against our inner judge, who keeps book on our shortcomings and transgressions. We need people to convince us that we are not as bad as we think we are."[1] Whereas the previous package focused on your mate's actions, this one focuses on who your mate is as a person. Consider packaging your words this way:

"I love you more than you could ever know . . ."
"Being married to you is fun, because you have such a great sense of humor . . ."
"I don't know what we would do without you around here . . .

Point Out What Was Done Right Before What Was Done Wrong

This may be the most direct application of Dennis Rainey's principle, "Catch your mate doing what's *right*." We all need a reminder of what we're doing well in the marriage. As one man said on our survey, "I need to be reminded at times that I get things RIGHT and how good my decisions are for the family." Pointing out the wrong is easy; here are some ways to remind your mate of what he did *right:*

"I can tell you really love the kids when . . ."

"I really appreciated it when you . . ."

"Thank you for going out of your way to . . ."

Find Fault Without Assigning Blame

James Walker writes, "If [a man] already sees himself as an incompetent because he carries a parental verdict about his imperfections, or if he watches a peer climb past him on the ladder of success, he will do whatever he can to avoid the pain of added disappointment."[2] Because men view life in terms of *status,* they often hear a complaint as an accusation of personal failure. They feel *blamed,* and they often avoid conflict as a consequence. To point out fault without assigning blame, try this:

"This is not all your fault . . ."

"I'm not angry with you, but something is bothering me . . ."

"I'm not blaming you; I'm just concerned about something . . ."

"I think there's something we need to do differently . . ."

Recognize Good Intentions Before Pointing Out Bad Actions

We have a rule in our house: No drinks allowed in the living room. Once, when Tim had just finished cutting the grass on a sweltering summer day, he was sitting in the living room when our son brought in a glass of water and spilled it on the sofa. Tim began to scold, "You *know* you're not supposed to bring water in here!" and our son began to cry. As it turned out, our son was bringing the glass of water to his father because he looked hot. Oops! The action may have been wrong, but the intention was excellent—as is often the case. You can recognize good intentions this way:

238

"I appreciate what you were trying to do . . ."

"I know you meant well . . ."

"I know this didn't come out the way you planned . . ."

These five packaging techniques may sound simple, but don't underestimate their potential for impact. Every time you repackage a negative statement in terms of the positive—every time you speak the truth *in love*—you neutralize the negative impact of the criticism.

Remember, the goal here is to choose a package *your* mate will like. What does your partner seem to appreciate most? Is it genuine praise, or expressions of approval, or recognition for her contributions to the family? Make sure you tailor the package to her specific needs and wants, and you'll find your words more warmly received.

Our first packaging principle is to make sure the package fits your *mate*. The second principle is similar . . .

Principle 2: Make Sure the Package Fits the Product

A rugged plastic jug with a handy spray pump should not be used for *Chanel*. A delicate crystal flute should not be used for *Pennzoil*. The package represents its contents, and a good package should fit the product it contains. We make three common mistakes when we're first learning the art and science of package design.

Package Too Small

"Speaking the truth in love" implies a *balance* between truth and love. Sometimes when we're first attempting to apply this principle, or when there has been a history of anger or friction, we're a little too sparing on the love: "Nice try. But next time . . ." It's a start, but you need to *expand*. *Why* was it a nice try? What did you appreciate about it? Why was it better than her last attempt? It takes a heaping helping of love to balance off a cold serving of truth.

Package Too Big

"You're a great mom, and I know you're trying, and I really love you, and I'm not blaming you, but would you clean the bathroom?" It's like wrapping a cassette tape in a refrigerator box, isn't it? "Speaking the truth in love" doesn't have to mean "giving a speech in love." When the package is too big, the gift inside is bound to be a disappointment. Jewelry boxes are small, but they seem to be *very* well received.

Package Too Obvious

A good rule of thumb is, "Never wrap a gift in cellophane." It sort of spoils the surprise. If your package is too transparent, your mate will see right through it. It lacks *genuineness.* If your package appears dishonest or manipulative, your mate will ignore the bait and simply wait for the hook that follows. "You are the world's greatest dad, BUT I wish you wouldn't shout at the kids," will simply come across as "Blah blah blah, I wish you wouldn't shout at the kids."

The key to genuineness is *sincerity.* We need to remind ourselves that speaking the truth in love is not just a euphemism for "buttering up your mate." This is not idle flattery or simply giving your words the right spin. Speaking the truth in love is first of all an attempt to correct your *own* perspective. To begin a complaint by saying, "You're a great mom and I appreciate everything you do around here," is to remind yourself that she *is* a great mom and that you have plenty to be thankful for. That change in perspective will keep you from exaggerating your complaint, and it will enable you to offer the praise with sincerity.

But no matter how good a package is, it needs to be changed from time to time. That's the third principle of package design.

Principle 3: Change the Package Often

As a little boy, Joy's brother Bill used a series of workbooks in school called "Think and Do." One day his parents asked him, "Billy, how do you like those 'Think and Do' books?"

"The Doin's okay," Billy said, "but that Thinkin's hard!"

Speaking the truth in love is an invitation to *think:* What is the truth in this situation, and what is the most loving way to say it? We all love formulas and rules because they save us the labor of having to think. But the minute we turn the principle of *speaking the truth in love* into a formula, it not only loses its power, but it also becomes counterproductive.

The first time you choose to introduce a complaint with a praise you may be very pleased with the results. Be careful! A formula mind-set might think, "Hey, that worked. I should do that again next time." And it might work the next time—but with slightly less impressive results. Once the approach begins to look like a formula, it loses its genuineness, and if it begins to feel manipulative, it will surely make your mate *angry.*

A *principle* mind-set would instead say, "Hey, that worked. What is the principle behind my words that made them effective? How can I apply that principle in a *different* way the next time?" If you'll think in terms of principles instead of formulas, you can continue to repackage your words in new and creative ways—and they will continue to have the positive impact you're hoping for.

The fourth principle of packaging applies when you're the one *receiving* a gift . . .

Principle 4: Take the Time to Admire a Beautiful Package

A beautifully wrapped package is a work of art, and art should be admired. Your mate doesn't *have* to take the time to package his words carefully, so when he does, it pays to notice. After all, speaking the truth in love is a step toward the fence, isn't it? And whenever your mate makes a move toward your world, it's important to "call to your mate across the fence" if you want to encourage him to move even closer. "Take the time to admire a nice package" is another way of saying, "Catch your mate *saying* what's right."

Speaking the truth in love requires awareness, discipline, and practice. That kind of effort deserves recognition. The next time your mate extends a beautifully wrapped gift to you, make sure she's aware that you noticed.

"Thank you for saying it that way . . ."

"That was a very thoughtful way of putting it . . ."

"I really appreciate you recognizing what I do around here . . ."

"I love it when you take the time to . . ."

We should not only *notice* one another; we should *learn* from one another. How did he say that? What was it you liked about it? How could you make it even better? What was his package telling you about the way *he* likes things packaged? We can learn the finer points of packaging design by studying one another. Is your mate a better natural communicator than you? Then observe the words she uses and the way she turns a phrase. What does she say that's especially effective? What can you learn from her?

By the way, here's a quick gift wrapping tip from Joy: Eliminate the words *nice* and *fine* from your vocabulary. In the world of gift wrapping, *nice* and *fine* are nothing but tissue paper. You can do better than that!

It's a funny thing about gifts: When one is received, there is a natural inclination to give one in return. The greatest benefit of speaking the truth in love is that it stimulates love in return. Couples who commit themselves to the art of good packaging discover that they have created an "upward spiral" in their communication. One good gift deserves another.

The fourth packaging principle reminded us to not only seek to speak the truth in love, but also to remember to reward our mates when they attempt to do the same. The fifth and final principle may seem obvious to you—but in our experience, the obvious is easily overlooked.

Principle 5: Deliver the Package!

Someone once said, "To love someone and not tell them is like wrapping a beautiful gift but never giving it away." Speaking the truth in love begins with a change in attitude, but it should not *end* there. This is far more than a new philosophy; this is a skill, and as with every skill, it's practice that makes perfect.

Don't wait for your next complaint to begin to communicate praise, approval, gratitude, and encouragement. These are powerful ways to repackage the truth with love, but they are powerful messages in themselves. If we wait until we have a negative message to enlist the help of praise and approval, our mates will begin to see praise and approval as nothing more than harbingers of bad news. We want our partners to be able to listen to our gratitude and encouragement without waiting for the other shoe to drop. We make this possible when we give these gifts away frequently and freely.

Love is an excellent package, but it's also a wonderful gift in itself. If we will not only speak the *truth* in love, but constantly give one another the *gift* of love, we may find that we have a lot less cold, hard truth to discuss at all.

* * *

A silversmith can turn a flat sheet of silver into a beautiful bowl with nothing but a small tool known as a planishing hammer. He holds the silver plate against a mushroom-shaped stake, and then he begins carefully but firmly to strike the silver with the hammer, working from the center outward in concentric circles.

Each time he strikes the silver it bends a tiny bit, but it also becomes more brittle. By the time he has covered the surface with hammer blows, the silver is so fragile that a single additional blow can fracture it. To avoid this, the silversmith heats the silver with a blowtorch until it begins to glow an orange-red. When this happens, the silver has regained its original softness and is ready to be molded once again.

This process, called *annealing,* is absolutely crucial to the shaping of metals—and it's crucial when working with human hearts as well. Every criticism from our mate, every angry complaint, every show of disapproval is like a blow from a hammer. We take the blow, and we bend a tiny bit, but we also become more brittle. As with metal, the danger is that we will take one blow too many and crack. "A man who hardens his neck after much reproof," Proverbs 29:1 cautions, "will suddenly be broken beyond remedy." If iron is to sharpen iron and not shatter it, an annealing process has to take place. Without it, the metal can be hammered, but not molded. In most marriages, there is too much hammering and too little molding taking place.

The book of Proverbs also reminds us that "a gentle answer turns away wrath" (15:1). Why does a *gentle* answer produce this deterrent effect? Why not a *correct* answer? The correct answer may be *accurate,* but the power to turn away wrath has more to do with style than substance. So does the power to shape and not destroy.

Annealing takes place in a marriage when couples—or even individuals—commit themselves to speak the truth in love. Truth is a hammer blow, but love is the gentle heat that keeps us malleable and makes it possible for us to receive it. If we are going to move toward the fence, if we are going to make progress in our areas of fundamental difference, then we need to think as much about the *way* we communicate as we do about the things we say. If the power of life and death are in the tongue, as Proverbs 18:21 says, then so is the power of love and forgiveness.

Now it's time to apply the principle of *moving toward the fence* to some specific situations. In the next two chapters we'll revisit each of the Seven Conflicts and show you how you can take a step closer to your mate's meadow in all of them.

244

For Chapter 14

Think of your words as a kind of *product,* something you hope to sell to your mate. Every product has to be packaged, and the package is critical to the product's success. Strangely, when it comes to marital communication, packaging is often ignored. The apostle Paul encourages us to "speak the truth in love." In communicating with our partners, truth should supply the *content,* and love should supply the *package.* It takes both, working together, to make a successful product. All of us need to become packaging experts, because in communication, as in manufacturing, packaging is everything. Five simple principles can help us become better packagers of the truth.

1. Choose a package your mate will like. Bringing up a complaint or a concern is sometimes a nasty business, so the goal is to look for the most diplomatic way to do it. Try to *introduce a complaint with a praise, express approval before disapproval, point out what was done right before what was done wrong, find fault without assigning blame, and recognize good intentions before pointing out bad actions.* The goal is to choose a package your mate will like. Tailor the package to her specific needs and wants, and you'll find that your words get a much better reception.

2. Make sure the package fits the product. We make three common errors when we're first learning the art of package design. Sometimes the *package is too small*—we're a little too sparing on our expression of praise or approval. Sometimes the *package is too big,* and then the gift inside is a bit of a disappointment. Sometimes the *package is too transparent,* and then our attempt to speak the truth in love looks like empty flattery or manipulation.

3. Change the package often. The first time you choose to introduce a complaint with a praise, you may be very pleased with the results. Be careful! We tend to think in formulas. A formula mind-set might reason, "Hey, that worked. I should do that again next time." And it might work the next time—but with slightly less impressive results. Once the approach begins to look like a formula, it loses its genuineness, and if it begins to feel manipulative, it's certain to make your mate *angry.*

4. Take the time to admire a beautiful package. A beautifully wrapped package is a work of art, and art should be admired. Speaking the truth in love requires awareness, discipline, and practice, and that kind of effort deserves recognition. The next time your mate extends a beautifully wrapped gift to you, make sure she's aware that you noticed. Try "Thank you for saying it that way," or, "That was a very thoughtful way of putting it."

5. Deliver the package! Someone once said, "To love someone and not tell them is like wrapping a beautiful gift but never giving it away." Speaking the truth in love begins with a change in attitude, but it should not *end* there. Don't wait for your next complaint to begin to communicate praise, approval, gratitude, and encouragement. Give away the gifts of gratitude and encouragement frequently and freely.

In the next two chapters we revisit each of the Seven Conflicts and suggest practical ways you can *move toward the fence.*

If you made it your goal to read all the Quick Takes in this book, congratulations! This is the final Quick Take, and you've fulfilled your goal. Now you understand the Seven Conflicts of marriage—but wouldn't you like to know how to resolve them? We strongly encourage you to read the next two chapters in full, where we'll revisit each of the Seven Conflicts and suggest practical ways you can *move toward the fence.*

CHAPTER fifteen

REVISITING the SEVEN CONFLICTS . . .

Security, Loyalty, and Responsibility

a n old Dutch proverb says, "He who is outside his door already has the hard part of his journey behind him." With most things in life, the hardest part is just getting started. The next two chapters describe the beginning of a lifelong journey. In the pages that follow we're going to revisit each of the Seven Conflicts and suggest some practical first steps you can take to begin to *move toward the fence* and *speak the truth in love.*

In chapter 12 we said that a critical first step is to *identify your dead ends,* to recognize your approaches to conflict resolution that *don't* work. As Will Rogers once said, "It's not what we don't know that hurts; it's what we know that ain't so." As we begin to revisit the Seven Conflicts, this would be a good time to remind you of six approaches that *never* work:

1. *Trying to talk her out of her dream, or into yours*
2. *Accusing him of being irrational because his dream doesn't make sense to **you***
3. *Arguing the greater virtue, logic, or practical benefit of **your** dream*
4. *Accusing her of overreacting because her dream means too much to her*
5. *Identifying five friends who do things **your** way*
6. *Accusing him of just being stubborn*

With those dead ends out of the way, let's describe some things that *do* work. In each of the sections that follow, we'll begin by encouraging you to consider both the assets and the potential liabilities of the dreams of Security, Loyalty, Responsibility, Caring, Order, Openness, and Connection. Each of these dreams is an excellent ambition, but each can have a dark side too—a dark side that can be avoided when we seek to achieve balance and avoid extremes.

For each of the Seven Conflicts, we'll give you two practical principles to get you started moving toward the fence—one for the spouse who holds the dream and one for the spouse who doesn't. Then we'll revisit some of the scenarios from chapters 3 through 9 to show you how things might have turned out differently with a different approach. We'll recommend fresh approaches in substance *and* style to maximize your chances for making new headway with the seven toughest conflicts in marriage.

SECURITY

The desire for Protection and Provision is an excellent dream—but when it goes too far, the dream has a dark side too.

The Good Side of Security	The Dark Side of Security
Safety	A fear of *all* risk-taking
Being well-equipped	Being overloaded
Minimizing risk	Minimizing options
Forethought and planning	Failing to trust in God's provision
Thinking of the future	Failing to enjoy today
Secure children	Overprotected children
Anticipating problems	Fear, worry, and anxiety
Spouse who feels protected	Spouse who feels limited

A Tip for the Non-Security-Minded

If Security is not your natural concern, what can you do to help satisfy your mate's greater desire for Protection and Provision? You can move toward the fence by *addressing Security before mentioning risk.*

We have a friend who once raced home to bring his wife some exciting news. All the way home he imagined her response—first her disbelief, then her gradual, astonished realization, and finally her overwhelming joy. He barely made it in the door before he blurted out the news.

"Guess what!" he said. "We're going to *China!*"

His wife just stood there, staring at him.

"Did you hear what I said? We're going to China for *two weeks!*"

There was a long pause, and then his wife slowly said, "What about the kids? Can they come too? We can't just leave them—who could watch them for two weeks? What about the dog? And who would take care of our house? It's the middle of the summer—someone would have to water the grass."

This time it was his turn to stare. "I can't believe you," he said. "I tell you that we have a chance to visit China, and all you can think about is watering the grass."

But she wasn't thinking about the grass—she was thinking about Security. She could be excited about the news, too, just as soon as she was sure that Protection and Provision were taken care of. China is great, but Security comes *first.*

Our friend realized later that he could have made things much easier for his wife if he had addressed her desires for Security *before* he brought up a potential risk. He might have said something more like this:

"I have some great news for you! I want you to know that this will affect the kids, and the dog, and the house—but I also want you to know that I've thought about all these things and we can take care of them. I know someone who can watch the kids, and I've taken care of the dog, and I've got the house covered. Are you ready? We're going to China!"

She may still have had *some* hesitation, and she still might have needed time to process all her concerns—but her husband would have gotten a lot better response if he had used this approach. The next time you want to suggest an activity that involves some risk—however slight the risk might appear to *you*—ask yourself, "Before I bring this up, how can I address my mate's desire for Security *first?*"

Let's revisit one of the scenarios from chapter 3 to see how this principle might have made a difference. Remember the husband and wife who were trying to enjoy a vacation together? *He* was enjoying himself, but *she* was not.

> He: *Isn't this a great vacation?*
> She: *Yeah. Great.*
> He: *How did you like the parasailing? Wasn't that incredible?*
> She: *Uh-huh. How much did that cost, anyway?*

Suppose instead that this husband applied the principle of *addressing Security before mentioning risk.* The conversation might have gone more like this:

> He: *Isn't this a great vacation?*
> She: *Yeah. Great.*
> He: *Look, I know that you're concerned about the finances. I want you to know that I've already thought it all through.*
> She: *You have?*
> He: *Yes, and I even made up a budget for us. I'd like us to do some things that are really different, even a little pricey—but I want you to know that we can*

*afford it, and we're not going to have to go into
debt. We can afford this.*

The wife would have been able to enjoy herself much
more if her husband had first addressed the financial plan for
the vacation. By addressing Security first, he could make it
possible for her to be more comfortable with risk.

A Tip for the Security-Minded

If Protection and Provision are your instinctive dream, how
can you maintain balance and avoid the dark side of Security?
How can you move toward the fence with your risk-taking
partner? A good way for the Security-minded to move toward
the fence is by *creating pockets of acceptable risk.*

Security is an excellent dream, but unbridled Security can
lead to a fear of *all* risk-taking. Without *some* openness to un-
certainty, no one would ever have children, change jobs, make an
investment, or travel more than a few miles from home. It all involves risk. We want our risk-taking partners to feel the freedom
to dream dreams and shoot for the stars, but we want our families
to be safe too. We want them to feel protected, but not *limited.*

Those who value Security can't be expected to simply "light-
en up," but they *can* look for areas in which they can feel free to
resist the natural impulse toward Protection and Provision. These
areas must be *within an overall safe environment*—that's why we
call them *pockets* of acceptable risk. As General Patton liked to
say, "Take *calculated* risks. That's not the same as being rash."

Suppose that the Security-minded wife in our scenario had
approached the vacation with our principle of *creating pockets
of acceptable risk.* Their conversation might have sounded
more like this:

He: *Isn't this a great vacation?*
She: *Yeah. Can I make a suggestion, though? There's one
way you could help me enjoy this vacation a lot more.*

He: Really? How?

She: You know that I worry about our finances some-times. Could we take a few minutes to decide how much we're going to spend on this vacation?

He: (Groan) You want to know what everything costs?

She: Not everything—just a bottom-line number, what-ever we agree we can afford. After that, as long as we stay under that number, anything goes.

He may still resist the idea of having to make a budget—but he would change his mind if he could see what a difference this simple step would make in his wife's attitude. Of course, it's better for both of them if they do this step *before* they go on vacation, but at this point the wife has realized the vacation is costing more than she thought it would, and she's finding it hard to relax and enjoy it. She can't ignore her desire for Security, but if she knows that they at least have a bottom line, then she's created a *pocket of acceptable risk.* Within that pocket, she could feel free to take a few chances—much to her husband's delight.

LOYALTY

There's no greater virtue than Loyalty, but even Loyalty has a dark side when it's taken to extremes.

The Good Side of Loyalty	The Dark Side of Loyalty
Faithful to a fault	Overlooking serious faults
Devoted to your mate	Idolizing your mate
Making your mate your priority	Ignoring all other priorities
Wanting your mate to be faithful	Jealousy and suspicion
Wanting to be your mate's priority	Selfishness and demanding

A Tip for Spouses of the Loyalty-Minded

If Loyalty is a bigger concern for your mate than it is for you, how can you begin to satisfy his desires for Faithfulness and Priority? A helpful way to demonstrate Loyalty to your mate is by *making a habit of offering accountability.*

As our children were growing up, we tried to impress upon them the difference between *trust* and *accountability.* We told them that we would always take them at their word. If our son said he would be at Todd's house, we trusted that that is where he would be. But if he left Todd's house to go to David's house instead, we asked him to call us and let us know of his change in plans. Our motive wasn't to constantly keep tabs on him or to track his every move. We didn't *distrust* him; it's just that there was always a chance that we might need to get in touch with him, and so we needed to know his whereabouts. It wasn't an issue of *trust;* it was an issue of *accountability.*

Instead of allowing your Loyalty-minded wife to struggle with vain imaginations, you can help fulfill her desires for Loyalty by *making a habit of offering accountability.* Instead of waiting for her to ask where you've been or why you were gone so long, tell her in advance. If you're going to be late for dinner, call first. If you have to make a stop on the way home, let her know. If an errand takes much longer than you expected, tell her why *before* she asks. By making a habit of doing these simple things, you are *offering accountability.* You are saying to her, "I have nothing to hide, and I have nothing to be ashamed of. I will live my life before you as an open book." Remember, *offering* accountability is the key. If she has to request it, it only feeds her imagination: "Why do I have to ask for this? What does he have to hide?"

We can offer accountability in other areas too. Tell your mate she's free to read your e-mail or check your Internet log. If you receive a personal letter, ask him if he'd like to see it. If she walks in just as you hang up the phone, tell her who you were talking to—don't wait for her to ask. Make a habit of *offering* accountability, and trust may be less of an issue in the future.

Another simple but powerful way to *offer accountability* is to remind your mate of your faithfulness. From time to time, look your Loyalty-minded mate in the eye and say, "I just want you to know that there is no one else. I am completely faithful to you, and I love only you." This may sound to you like stating the obvious—that's because Loyalty is not your issue. Your Loyalty-minded mate *wants* to trust you, and you can help relieve those nameless fears and nagging doubts by simply reminding her of your love and commitment.

Let's apply the principle of *offering accountability* to a scenario we saw in chapter 4 . . .

She: Where have you been?

He: At the hardware store. Why?

She: All this time? You've been gone for three hours.

He was gone longer than she expected, and a Loyalty conflict is under way. But if he had applied the principle of *offering accountability,* the conversation might have taken a much different turn.

She: Where have you been?

He: At the hardware store. I know I was gone longer than I said I'd be, but I got to looking at power tools, and I started reading some of the instruction manuals. I stopped for gas, and then I came straight home. Sorry if you were worried about me —I'll try to call next time.

It was a simple thing, but by showing a willingness to reveal his whereabouts—by *offering* accountability—he protected his Loyalty-minded wife from doubt and suspicion.

A Tip for the Loyalty-Minded

If Faithfulness and Priority *are* especially important to you, what can you do to avoid the extremes of jealousy, possessiveness, or suspicion? What can you do to move toward the fence? A helpful first step is to begin to *voice gratitude and appreciation for faithfulness.*

As we said in chapter 4, those who especially value Loyalty are sometimes vulnerable to doubt and thoughts of suspicion. You can help resist the temptation of suspicion by reminding yourself of your mate's track record of faithfulness—and even more important, by thanking him for it.

First Thessalonians 5:18 (NIV) tells us to "give thanks in all circumstances"—not to merely *feel* gratitude, but to *express* it. Something about thanksgiving transforms doubt and reinforces hope. Remember, suspicion grows best in a vacuum —wherever there is an absence of knowledge or encouragement. By giving thanks, we constantly fill the vacuum of doubt with reminders of past Loyalty.

And don't forget, thanksgiving has a transforming effect on both the giver *and* the receiver. By expressing gratitude to your mate for his Faithfulness and Priority, you make it much easier for him to hear your occasional doubts. As more than one man commented on our survey, "I need to hear what I'm doing *right* before I can hear what I'm doing *wrong.*"

Let's return to our scenario again. Instead of raising concerns about Loyalty, what if the wife had instead tried to *voice gratitude and appreciation for faithfulness?* How could things have gone differently?

She: Where have you been?

He: At the hardware store. Why?

She: Look, I don't mean to doubt you. One of the things I appreciate most about you is your faithfulness.

*I've always been able to trust you, and I can't tell
you how important that is to me. It's just that these
thoughts cross my mind sometimes . . .*

He: *I'm sorry I was gone so long. I'll call next time.*

RESPONSIBILITY

Some of us feel a strong desire to be Responsible. But what
happens when a sense of Obligation and Expectation go too far?

THE GOOD SIDE OF RESPONSIBILITY	THE DARK SIDE OF RESPONSIBILITY
Valuing the opinions of others	Ruled by the opinions of others
Submitting to proper authority	Yielding to any authority
Principle-oriented	Rule-bound
Sense of right and wrong	Sees only black and white
Polite and mannerly	Formal and rigid
Fulfilling obligations	Acting only out of obligation

A Tip for the Responsibility-Minded

If you possess a strong sense of Obligation and Expectation, it's important to avoid the extreme of being *bound* by rules or the opinions of others. You can take a step away from that extreme and toward the fence by applying this principle: *Tell your mate what you want, not what he ought to do.*

Remember, the Responsibility conflict occurs when one partner feels a sense of Obligation or Expectation that the other does not. The solution is not to try to create the same sense of Responsibility in your partner—that may be impossible to do. The solution is to help your mate understand how important your sense of Obligation is to *you.*

Instead of telling our partners how we feel about their behavior, we sometimes make the tactical error of trying to convince them of the authority of our unwritten rule—but that only makes the problem worse. Instead of arguing about the reasonableness of the rule, or why it's important to obey, or listing friends and acquaintances who follow the rule, a more useful approach is to simply *tell your mate what you want.* Even if your mate doesn't share your sense of Obligation or Expectation, he still has a desire to please *you.*

Let's go back to a scenario of a couple's conversation from chapter 5. Their neighbors the Andersons are moving Saturday, and the wife thinks they *ought* to help.

> *She:* The Andersons are moving this Saturday.
>
> *He:* Oh?
>
> *She:* They're moving themselves, you know. We should offer to help.
>
> *He:* Did they ask for our help?
>
> *She:* You don't wait for people to ask. You offer to help.

Now let's apply our principle: *Tell your mate what you want, not what he ought to do . . .*

> *She:* The Andersons are moving this Saturday.
>
> *He:* Oh?
>
> *She:* They're moving themselves, you know. We should offer to help.
>
> *He:* Did they ask for our help?
>
> *She:* I really want to offer to help. I think they expect us to, and even if they don't, I'll feel really embarrassed if we don't even offer. Would you please come with me on Saturday? It doesn't have to be all day—just a couple of hours.

Even with this approach we can't guarantee that he'll jump at the opportunity to help. But we *can* guarantee that his wife will get a lot further than she would by arguing that her husband *ought* to help. Because his dream is not Responsibility, *ought* will not spur him to action—but his wife's feelings just might.

A Tip for Spouses of the Responsibility-Minded

If Obligation and Expectation mean more to your mate than to you, here's a first step to help you move toward her Responsible world. It's a derivative of the principle we just suggested to your mate: *Think about pleasing your mate, not obeying a rule.*

If you're not especially motivated by Obligation or a sense of what other people expect of you, what *does* motivate you? If you're like most people, you're motivated by a desire to please your mate. That's good—and that's the beginning of a solution to your Responsibility conflicts. Instead of endlessly debating whether you *should* or *shouldn't* do something, why not change your focus? Think about pleasing your mate instead of obeying a rule.

Think again about the Andersons and moving day. His wife believes they ought to help, but he feels no such Obligation, and now a Responsibility conflict is under way. But suppose he responded to his wife's sense of Obligation in a different way . . .

> She: *The Andersons are moving this Saturday.*
> He: *Oh?*
> She: *They're moving themselves, you know. We should offer to help.*
> He: *Did they ask for our help?*
> She: *You don't wait for people to ask. You offer to help.*

He: *Wait a minute. You like to help out whenever some-one is in need. We can't help everybody, so what I'd like to know is, how important is this to you?*

She: *I know I tend to volunteer a lot, but the Andersons are our neighbors. I'll really feel embarrassed if we don't at least offer to help. This is very important to me.*

Once again, there's no guarantee that her husband will be lending a hand on moving day. But there's a much better chance, because this approach put the request in completely different terms. Instead of asking himself, "*Should* I help?" he's now asking, "Am I willing to do what's very important to my wife?" This is the impact of the principle, *Think about pleasing your mate, not obeying a rule.*

These are some practical steps to get you started moving toward the fence in the areas of Security, Loyalty, and Responsibility. In the next chapter, we'll revisit the dreams of Caring, Order, Openness, and Connection.

CHAPTER SIXTEEN

Revisiting the seven conflicts . . .

Caring, Order, Openness, and Connection

CARING

The world is a better place because of Caring people—but believe it or not, even Caring has a dark side when it's taken to extremes.

THE GOOD SIDE OF CARING	THE DARK SIDE OF CARING
Aware of the feelings of others	Vain imaginations
Shows appreciation	Shows appreciation to get appreciation
Cares even for strangers	Overextends at family's expense
Helps without being asked	Helps without being wanted
Puts her own needs second	Loses touch with her own needs
Cares how everyone is doing	Lacks healthy boundaries
Cares about details	Controlling or smothering

A Tip for Those Who Value Caring

If Awareness and Initiative come easily for you, and if you'd like more Caring from your mate, then do yourself a favor by *teaching your mate how to care.*

In chapter 6 we said that we want our partners to notice things on *their* own. We don't want to always have to *tell* them. Having to ask "How do I look?" takes all the satisfaction out of any compliment that might follow. So why should you have to *teach your mate how to care?* Doesn't that have exactly the same effect?

We're not advising that you tell your mate *what* to say— just *how* to say it. Caring conflicts begin when your partner fails to care, or when your partner doesn't express care *the way you want.* That's when it helps to explain to your mate what Caring looks like to you.

A man says to his wife, "That's a nice dress." He thinks that his comment shows Awareness, and by voicing his opinion he has taken the Initiative. If that's not Caring, what is? But from his wife's perspective, his expression of Caring leaves a lot to be desired. First of all, "nice" is an empty shell of a word—it means nothing at all. He might as well have said, "That dress is adequate." And second, his comment was not about her; it was about a *dress.* Would the dress have looked just as nice to him if it were hanging on a rack? It would be much better to say, "*You* look beautiful *in* that dress." With just two minor adjustments he would have had a real compliment there. They're great ideas—so why doesn't she tell him?

The reason we don't teach our mates how to care is that we tell ourselves we shouldn't have to. It's true, you shouldn't have to tell your husband to care—that's his responsibility— but you do have to tell him *how* to care if you want him to Initiate in the way that you most appreciate.

Remember the scenario from chapter 6, where the wife had to ask her husband how she looked?

She: I hate to have to ask this, but how do I look?
He: You look great.
She: Thanks a lot.

He: *I said you look great. What's wrong with that?*
She: *What's wrong is that I have to ask you.*

Now suppose she made the decision to *teach her mate how to care.* Her response might have been more like this:

She: *I hate to have to ask this, but how do I look?*
He: *You look great.*
She: *I appreciate the compliment, but can I tell you something? If I have to ask you, your compliment doesn't really mean anything to me. I like it when you comment on specific things about my hair, or my clothes, or my body. That tells me you notice when I change things day to day.*

One quick lesson in Awareness and Intitiative isn't going to turn him into Mr. Caring overnight, and there's still no telling when his next compliment will come, so don't give up if you have to remind him again. But chances are his next admiring comment will be a little more satisfying than "Nice dress."

A Tip for Spouses of the Caring

If you know that your mate puts a high value on Caring, then you need to look for your own ways to move toward the fence. Remember that Caring consists of Awareness and Initiative, so a first step in either area will be well received. We'd like to suggest a principle in the area of Initiative: *Make a practice of taking first steps.*

The word *initiate* means "to get things going by taking the first step." Those who value Caring are often burdened by the need to "get things going." They look at their homes, their children, their marriages, and they see a dozen areas where someone needs to just take the first step, and they feel that the duty always seems to fall to them. This is where our principle comes into play. To help relieve the burden from your Caring partner, *make a practice of taking first steps.*

Here's the secret that makes it all possible: To take the first step, you don't have to know what the second step is. The trick is to just get things rolling; it's easier to steer a moving car than a parked one. Once you get things going, you can figure out your next steps as you go.

Let's revisit another scenario from chapter 6. Remember this one?

> *She: Can I talk to you about something?*
> *He: Sure.*
> *She: A month ago we talked about how the kids need to learn more about the Bible.*
> *He: Right. I remember.*
> *She: That's not really important to you, is it?*
> *He: What do you mean? Of course that's important to me.*

He *does* care—or so he says. But his Caring failed to impress his wife because his Awareness wasn't matched with Initiative. But suppose he's beginning to *make a practice of taking first steps.* In that case, the scenario might have gone more like this:

> *She: Can I talk to you about something?*
> *He: Sure.*
> *She: A month ago we talked about how the kids need to learn more about the Bible.*
> *He: I remember. The problem is, I don't know much about the Bible. So here's what I did: I went down to that Christian bookstore, and they recommended this family devotional book. They said I could read*

> *a little of it each night at the dinner table, and then*
> *we could all talk about it. I thought that's how we*
> *could start.*
>
> She: *That would be terrific!*

His efforts may not sound like much, but to her it was *terrific*—because it's one area of life where she won't have to initiate. He's not sure what his next step will be, but for now it doesn't matter; the important thing is that he's taken his first step toward the fence, and his first step toward real Caring.

ORDER

Structure and Control can help make Order out of chaos—but when Order goes too far, it creates a chaos of its own.

THE GOOD SIDE OF ORDER	THE DARK SIDE OF ORDER
Organized	Controlling
Efficient	Impersonal
Structured	Obsessive
Scheduled	Inflexible
Punctual	Impatient
Hands-on	Perfectionistic

A Tip for the Orderly

If Structure and Control are important values to you, you can effectively resist the tendency to become controlling or obsessive by *focusing on critical areas only.*

The problem with the dream of Order is that it can become all-encompassing. Order is not just the desire for a neater household; it's a way of looking at life—the view that *everything* works better with Structure and Control. It may be true that every area of your marriage and family could benefit from additional Order, but not every area is equally important. You can take a major step away from the world of the obsessive if you can distinguish areas where Order is *critical* from areas where it's only *desirable*.

In chapter 7 we described a situation where an Orderly husband was searching with great frustration for his wife's Visa receipts. Their conversation went like this:

> *He:*   *I can't find your Visa receipts—again.*
>
> *She:*   *They're right over there.*
>
> *He:*   *Where?*
>
> *She:*   *On my desk. Look under that newspaper.*
>
> *He:*   *Your desk is a disaster! You need to keep this clean. You're supposed to put your Visa receipts in this box, remember?*

She finds the receipts, but her desk is a disaster. It's *always* a disaster, which drives his Ordered mind to distraction. This would be a good time for him to try out the principle of *focusing on critical areas only*.

> *He:*   *I can't find your Visa receipts—again.*
>
> *She:*   *They're right over there.*
>
> *He:*   *Where?*
>
> *She:*   *On my desk. Look under that newspaper.*
>
> *He:*   *You know, your desk is your business, but there are certain areas where we need to be better organized. I'm especially concerned about the credit card receipts—I need to reconcile the bill at the end of the month. I'll make a deal with you: If you'll agree to put your credit card receipts in this box, you can do whatever you want with the rest of your desk. Deal?*

What does she have to lose? By *focusing on critical areas only,* he set up a crucial Structure while requiring only a minimal adjustment on her part. He moved toward her world without surrendering the critical part of his own.

A Tip for the Less-than-Orderly

If your mate's desires for Structure and Control are making you feel like Oscar Madison from the *Odd Couple,* why not move toward her fence? One way to satisfy both her preference for Order and your desire for spontaneity is by *planning to be disorganized.*

As we said in chapter 7, we've often disagreed over our approaches to leisure time. One of us likes a schedule and a plan, and one of us likes to take things as they come. For years it seemed like a case of terminal gridlock—until it suddenly dawned on us that we could fulfill *both* of our desires by simply *planning to be disorganized.*

Now when free time comes along, we make a schedule—but within that schedule we allow times that are unstructured. We specifically schedule times that *have* no schedule, times when we will do whatever we want whenever we want to. By *planning to be disorganized,* we satisfy our desires for both Order and spontaneity.

The same principle applies to other situations as well. In chapter 7 we described a Structured husband and a spontaneous wife on a mission together to buy a birthday present . . .

He: *Let's head to the mall first. When we get there we'll split up and hit the big department stores first. We'll each make a list of possible gift ideas, then we'll meet by the food court in half an hour to compare lists and decide where to go to make the final purchase.*

She: *I hate shopping with you.*

If they had only *planned to be disorganized,* their excursion might have gone more like this:

> He: *Let's head to the mall first. When we get there we'll split up and . . .*
>
> She: *Hold it a minute. I hate shopping that way. Can we compromise? Let's do it like this: You can decide which stores we'll visit, and you can even decide the order of events. But once we get to the store, then we do it my way. No lists, no deadlines, no schedule —okay?*

It's not exactly what he wanted, but by *planning to be disorganized* they managed to satisfy both of their desires—and they both moved toward the fence in the process.

OPENNESS

Everyone loves a Sociable person, but even Openness has its liabilities when it's taken to an extreme.

THE GOOD SIDE OF OPENNESS	THE DARK SIDE OF OPENNESS
Many friends	Superficial friends
Loves people	Hates tasks
Loves company	Avoids solitude
Wants to be included	Manipulates to be included
Treasures friends	Ignores spouse
Motivated by groups	Lacks individual discipline

A Tip for Open Personalities

If you thrive in social situations and feel energized by people, it's hard to understand a mate who constantly seeks time to be alone. You can take a giant first step toward the fence if you will *make sure she has time to recharge.*

Statistically, 75 percent of people are Open personalities; they enjoy Sociability and draw Energy from interaction with others. What a great personality trait—who wouldn't want to be considered Sociable? But try as they might, introverts are exhausted by people and require time to recharge alone—though their desire for seclusion is sometimes a source of guilt. Keirsey and Bates write, "Introverts have reported that they have gone through much of their lives believing that they *ought* to want more sociability. . . . As a result, the introvert seldom provides adequately for his very legitimate desire for territoriality, for breathing room, without experiencing a vague feeling of guilt."[1]

You can relieve your mate's feelings of guilt or shame simply by recognizing that her desire for breathing room is not selfishness, or snobbery, or social awkwardness. It is a "very legitimate desire for territoriality." It's critical to remember that introverts like people too—but because people drain them of Energy, they need time to recharge before they're ready to face people again.

Remember this situation from chapter 8? A husband and wife were thinking ahead to the upcoming weekend . . .

He: *What a week! I'm exhausted.*
She: *Me too. I can't wait for the weekend.*
He: *I've got an idea . . . Let's get the whole gang together on Saturday and head for the beach.*
She: *(Groan) I thought you said you were tired.*

He's ready for a party, and she's ready to collapse. This would be a good time for this Sociable husband to move toward the fence . . .

He: *I've got an idea . . . Let's get the whole gang togeth-er on Saturday and head for the beach.*

She: *(Groan) I thought you said you were tired.*

He: *I forgot—you've been doing employee reviews all week, haven't you? You need some down time. How about this: Friday night is all yours. I'll unplug the phone, and you can have the apartment all to your-self. Then we can talk about Saturday, okay?*

If you want to encourage your mate to be more Sociable, then *make sure she has time to recharge.* In the process, you just might recognize your own need for a little "alone time" too.

A Tip for Spouses of Open Personalities

If Sociability is not your natural instinct, and if people have a way of tiring you out, then you can take your first step toward the fence by *seeking to expand your boundaries.*

In chapter 13 we described the problem of *polarization,* the tendency to alter your personality in response to your mate. Nowhere is this tendency more common than with the issue of Openness. *He* continually seeks the company of others, so *she* persistently seeks to withdraw. He can't wait to get out of the house, so she can't wait to get home. They both want to recharge, but neither one feels energized because they've polar-ized. They've faced off over their respective needs and desires, and now they're involved in an endless tug-of-war that neither one can win.

A tug-of-war is a struggle to pull away from one another —but the struggle always ends when one partner decides to step *forward.* That's what moving toward the fence is all about. You can put an end to your tug-of-war over Openness by *seeking to expand your boundaries.*

When you look ahead to the weekend, your natural pref-erence might be to spend Friday night curled up alone with a good book. Instead, why not suggest dinner with another couple? Not a party or a huge group gathering, and not an entire evening in the company of others. Just dinner. And when you see a free evening coming, why not recommend inviting the neighbors over for dessert? Not *all* the neighbors, just one other couple, and not even for dinner this time—just for dessert.

These are small steps, and they certainly won't satisfy all the social desires of your people-hungry mate. But they *will* let him know that you are not a recluse, that you like people, too, and that you're willing to move toward the fence.

Let's return to the couple who were attempting to plan a weekend outing at the beach. If you remember the end of the dialogue, you probably noticed that they didn't get very far. They ended up as they always do, in a tug-of-war over their different desires for Openness.

> *He:*   *I've been sitting in my cubicle chained to my desk all week. This would be a great way to recharge!*
>
> *She:*   *But I spent the whole week doing employee reviews. I've been meeting with people for five straight days. I just want to be alone.*
>
> *He:*   *C'mon, you could stand one more day of people.*
>
> *She:*   *And you could stand one more day alone.*

But suppose the woman made a conscious choice to put an end to the tug-of-war by choosing to expand her boundaries ever-so-slightly. She might have said something like this:

> *He:*   *C'mon, you could stand one more day of people.*
>
> *She:*   *I'm not sure I could stand a whole **group** of people. Can I make a suggestion? Let's just invite one other couple to come along. How about Joe and Lisa? We know them well. As tired as I am, I'd rather not invite a lot of strangers. How does that sound?*

He wanted to get the whole gang together, and she suggests just Joe and Lisa. It may not sound like much, but it's a lot better than saying in her best Greta Garbo voice, "I want to be *alone.*" By *seeking to expand your boundaries* to include other people, just a few people at a time, you can begin to relieve the tug-of-war and conserve your Energy at the same time.

CONNECTION

As we said before, Connection conflicts are sometimes the worst because they underlie all of the other arguments. It's hard to resolve a disagreement when you can't even make a good Connection. Every style of Communication and Decision Making has a dark side associated with it.

The Style of Connection	The Dark Side of This Style of Connection
Linear communicator	Boring
Circular communicator	Distracted
Cognitive communicator	Passionless
Emotional communicator	Impulsive
Didactic communicator	Rigid
Interactive communicator	Rude
Decisive decision maker	Impetuous
Tentative decision maker	Vacillating
Intuitive decision maker	Biased
Evidential decision maker	Rationalistic
Final decision maker	Inflexible
Open-ended decision maker	Noncommittal

Tips for Different Kinds of Communicators

Once you've identified your own natural style of Communication, it's important to begin to communicate in a way that your spouse can appreciate—important, that is, if you really want to make a Connection.

A *linear communicator* can remind himself what conversation is *for.* For him, the purpose of conversation is information, but for her the purpose is *interaction.* Instead of pushing ahead for the facts, he can stop and ask himself, "Do we understand each other? Are we making a good Connection?"

A *circular communicator* can learn to begin with a summary statement: "Yes, I saw Johnny's teacher today, and Johnny has to stay after school tomorrow because he failed his math test." With the facts in hand, the linear partner can now sit back and more easily enjoy the ride.

No one would think it unreasonable if his mate asked him to speak louder or more clearly. Volume and clarity are two qualities that make a message intelligible; emotion can help too. A *cognitive communicator's* message would come through a lot clearer if he would tell his emotional partner not only what he thinks, but how he feels. He can begin to practice the discipline of asking himself, "How do I *feel* about this?"

Emotional communicators can help their cognitive partners by helping them recognize their emotions. After they give you the facts, ask some questions. "How do you feel?" is a little too frontal; instead, try "How does that strike you?" or even "What do you think about that?" By asking him what he thinks *about* his thoughts, his emotions might begin to enter the picture too.

Didactic communicators can resist the temptation to deliver a lecture by interrupting themselves. Instead of waiting to be interrupted and then becoming impatient or frustrated, they can break up their own monologue with questions or requests for feedback. "What do you think?" "Do you know what I mean?"

273

Interactive communicators can let their partners know they have a question or comment without actually interrupting the conversation—at least, not for long. "Remind me to ask you something," is another way of saying, "I'd like to interject something here, but I know you don't like to be interrupted, so I'll save it until you're finished."

Tips for Different Kinds of Decision Makers

Regardless of your style of Decision Making, there's always some way to move toward the fence.

Decisive and *tentative* decision makers can agree together in advance on a deadline for a decision. The deadline allows the decisive partner to know that there will be an eventual end to her tentative partner's procrastination, and it gives the tentative partner the freedom to think things over without feeling pressured or hurried. It also helps the decisive partner to *lighten up;* there's no sense trying to hurry things along when the decision isn't due for another week.

Intuitive and *evidential* decision makers can discuss in advance how their decision will be made. By focusing on the decision itself, rather than on what the decision will be, they can make sure they allow room for both evidence and intuition. They can decide what research will be helpful, who will gather it, and what the limits of their fact-gathering will be. They can agree as to when the research phase will be over and when the decision making can begin.

Final and *open-ended* decision makers have no problem agreeing to *make* a decision; their problem is agreeing about the decision once it's *done*. Final decision makers can agree to a review period, sort of like a thirty-day money-back guarantee on a purchase. The open-ended partner has thirty days to agonize, reflect, and reconsider a decision—after that, it's done. In this way, second-guessing becomes an intentional part of the decision-making process itself.

CHapter seventeen

marriage to a difficult man—or woman

S arah Edwards was married to a rather unusual man. Her husband Jonathan had enrolled at Yale University in 1716 at the tender age of thirteen and graduated four years later as valedictorian of his class. He was a brilliant man, a constant student with very few friends and no social life to speak of. He was a pastor, a theologian, a philosopher, and an evangelist who traveled for weeks at a time, leaving Sarah to care for the farm and eleven children. It's no surprise that when Sarah's own biography was finally written, it was entitled *Marriage to a Difficult Man.*

In one way or another, we're *each* married to a difficult man or woman. Your mate may not be a reclusive philosophical genius, but he or she still has enough quirks, oddities, and idiosyncrasies to merit the label "difficult."

Maybe a better word would be "eccentric." The word *eccentric* literally means "off-center." The planets rotate around our sun in *eccentric* orbits. Applied to a person, *eccentric* suggests the idea of odd or unconventional behavior. As the dictionary puts it, "see synonyms at *strange.*"

All of us are strange in our own ways. When Tim was in college, he shared a house with a man who used to mix all of his food together before eating it. Meatloaf, corn, and applesauce, all stirred together into an unrecognizable glop. "Why not?" he used to say. "It all goes to the same place." There is a logic to his words—a bizarre, twisted logic—but the fact remains, that kind of behavior won't get a person invited out to dinner very often. It's just too eccentric.

As we grow up, each of us collects a jumbled closet full of strange habits and peculiarities. You can live out of that closet as a single person, because there's no one to challenge your eccentricity. But a strange thing happens when marriage comes along. For the first time, someone *cares* if you wear your shirts inside out. Someone is there to *disagree* with you, to *correct* you, to be *offended* by you, because you are now a reflection on her. When you marry, your life is given a new relational center.

The truth is, we all liked some of our old eccentricities, and we resent having to give them up just because of a husband or wife. We liked staying up until four in the morning and then sleeping until noon. We enjoyed eating Cap'n Crunch cereal for dinner whenever we pleased. We loved living without a budget, wearing whatever we pleased, and cleaning the apartment only when it was time to move out. But in a marriage, two eccentric people move in together. Now one of you is a night owl and one of you is a morning dove. One of you eats Little Debbie Cosmic Crispy Bars, and one of you eats only organically grown vegetables. One of you is the life of the party, and one of you is the party pooper.

When we say "I do" we're both given a new center, and marriage is a process of correcting our individual orbits to revolve around that new axis. We go from being *eccentric* to *concentric*. Our orbits will never be identical, but if they share the same center, at least they can align. That realignment is a lifelong process, and sometimes a painful one, but it's a healthy process too. Through that shifting of orbits, God keeps us from becoming *extreme people*.

What's wrong with being extreme? After all, isn't it our quirks and oddities that make us interesting? Isn't variety the spice of life? When we marry, are we all supposed to surrender our uniquenesses and assume the roles of cookie-cutter husbands and Stepford wives? Do we all have to become *bland?*

The goal is not to become bland, but *balanced.* Biographies of famous men and women are often the stories of extreme people. In many cases, it was their very *lack* of balance that made them great. But their extremeness didn't always contribute to their happiness—or the happiness of those who had to live with them. Jean Jacques Rousseau was a philosopher and social theorist who helped lay the groundwork for the French Revolution. He was also a musician, a botanist, and a prolific writer. To make more time for his work, Rousseau placed all of his children in an orphanage—a horrific environment for a child in eighteenth-century France. Rousseau had many fans, but it's doubtful that his children were among them.

We don't need to go back to the eighteenth century to find examples of extreme people. We don't need to go anywhere at all. We're *all* extreme people in one way or another—and we would be even more extreme if not for the balancing influence of our partners.

Everyone has strengths and weaknesses. One of the most crucial things to understand about ourselves is that our strengths and weaknesses are related. *Every strength, left unchecked, becomes a weakness.* Samson was enormously strong; he became violent and impulsive. King David was passionate and expressive; he became lustful and promiscuous. All of us, left to ourselves, tend to become more and more extreme. Maybe that's why Eric Hoffer once wrote, "A man by himself is in bad company."[1]

In this book we've encouraged you to ask yourself some hard questions. What are your dreams? What is your essential form? Where do you stand on the issues of Security, Loyalty, Responsibility, Caring, Order, Openness, and Connection? Some of these issues you first became aware of through conflict with your mate. You didn't even know that you cared about Security until you realized that your mate doesn't value it *at all.* Marriage isn't just a lifetime of getting to know another person; it's also a lifetime of getting to know *yourself*—and that knowledge isn't always pleasant. As a young man once said to us, "I had no idea how selfish I was until I got married. Now I know—and now *she* knows too. "

When we begin to realize how very different we are from one another, we instinctively conclude that our partner must be somehow *damaged.* After all, it can't be me. *I'm* the way people are *supposed* to be. What's *her* problem? Then we begin the search for ways to put our mate back in proper working order. Keirsey and Bates write:

> Seeing others around us differing from us, we conclude that these differences in individual behavior are but temporary manifestations of madness, badness, stupidity, or sickness. In other words, we rather naturally account for variations in the behavior of others in terms of flaw and affliction. Our job, at least for those near us, would seem to be to correct these flaws. Our Pygmalion project, then, is to make all those near us just like us.[2]

The problem is not that I'm disorganized; the problem is that *you* are a neat freak. The problem is not that I'm an extrovert; the problem is that *you* don't like people. We instinctively see our mate's differences as evidence of some shortcoming, and then we busy ourselves with the task of making him the person he *ought* to be. But marriage is not a license to recreate your mate in your own image—that would just be multiplying error. Marriage is a chance to cooperate with God's plan to recreate *both* of you in the image of His Son.

You may have been hoping that within these pages you would find some tip or technique that would solve your marital disagreements once and for all. We'd like to remind you of something we wrote in the introduction of this book: "If your goal is to eliminate all conflict from your marriage, we can't help you. We believe that conflict is an inevitable part of *every* marriage. While the *amount* of conflict in marriage can certainly be reduced, and the *experience* of conflict can be greatly improved, the basic message of this book is that some conflicts *will not go away*—but you can learn to understand them and deal with them in a way that will allow you to love your mate more than ever." That's the bottom line: Conflict will not go away, but you can love each other anyway.

We'd like to leave you with one final principle—a principle that we encourage you to keep foremost in your mind as you leave this book and attempt to love your partner even in the midst of disagreement. It may be the most important principle of all . . .

Don't Live with Conflict; Live with Your Mate

What does this enigmatic principle mean? It's a kind of "riddle within a riddle," and we'd like to offer three clues to help clarify its meaning.

Clue 1: Don't View Your Marriage in Terms of Your Problems

The United Nations estimates that there are 110 *million* land mines planted somewhere on our planet. If you live in America, that's an interesting bit of trivia—but if you live in Cambodia or Angola, it's a way of life. It must be awkward for the Cambodian Department of Tourism to proudly proclaim, "Our country is beautiful, peaceful, and secure—just be careful where you step." If you've roped off significant minefields within your marriage, you may no longer view your relationship as beautiful, peaceful, and secure. You may see it as *explosive*.

Everyone has a mental image of his or her marriage. For some, the picture is one of general pleasure and satisfaction—it just has a few problems. For others, the picture is one big problem. When there is anger and unresolved conflict, there is a tendency to repaint the landscape of our marriage so that our problems dominate the entire canvas. We are a problem couple, and this is a troubled marriage.

The problem is, that negative mental image tends to dominate any new positive element that enters into it. When you were first married, you saw yourselves as a happy couple. When a problem came along, you were a happy couple with a problem. But when that mental image becomes predominantly negative, the opposite occurs. If you see your marriage in terms of your problems, even if you or your partner tries to change for the better, you will see those efforts as exceptions to the rule. Michele Weiner-Davis writes:

> When a marriage has been on the rocks for some time, a *series* of positive experiences are required to convince a couple that the marriage is on safer ground. One mutually satisfying experience is often viewed as a fluke unless it is followed by several other satisfying experiences. In contrast to this, if two weeks of harmony are followed by a single antagonistic episode, it completely negates the two harmonious weeks which preceded it. It is as if the two good weeks never happened. Our "here-we-go-again" mind-set filters out the positive experiences.[3]

We have to be careful to guard ourselves against that "'here-we-go-again' mind-set [that] filters out the positive experiences." If we don't, we let our discouragement over the past become a self-fulfilling prophecy of the future. A regrettable past is bad enough; a past that is allowed to control the future is far worse.

At a marriage conference, a woman came up to us with such a long list of complaints about her husband that we finally had to interrupt. "Why did you marry him?" we asked. She stared at us for a minute in surprise, and then she said, "Well, he wasn't such a jerk when I married him."

Of course he wasn't. He was a kind, loving, thoughtful, generous man—the same man *every* woman marries. But her mental painting of him had changed—maybe for some good reasons—so that the image she now held in her mind was labeled "Portrait of a Jerk." But suppose her husband genuinely decides to try to "move toward the fence." How would the woman view her husband's change of heart? Her mental painting might prove unalterable. Only the label would change to read "Jerk Moving Toward a Fence."

That's why we encourage couples to try to recall their *original* paintings. When Jesus spoke to the church at Ephesus, he instructed them to "remember from where you have fallen" (see Revelation 2:5). That's good advice for all of us. Why were you originally attracted to this man or woman? What were the person's qualities *then?* What was the mental picture you carried with you as a newlywed? Believe it or not, the person you're now married to is the same person in that original painting. She may have been retouched, or covered over with subsequent layers of paint, but it's still her. Maybe all she needs to have the courage to change is the reminder that you are ready to think the best of her. She needs to know if you're still willing to repaint the picture.

For some of you, your original image of your mate was a work of fiction. Perhaps she was secretly an alcoholic, or perhaps he disguised an uncontrollable temper. You never discovered those parts of your mate's personality until after you were married—or perhaps you did see hints of them, but in your eagerness and infatuation you chose to overlook them. What good does it do for you to recall your original painting? It was a forgery! Nevertheless, our principle still applies: We cannot let our discouragement over the past *or* the present become a self-fulfilling prophecy of the future. By the grace of God your mate *is* capable of change—but you'll never recognize that change unless you're willing to believe it can happen.

Your marriage is troubled—so is ours. Your marriage is also wonderful—so is ours. We have to remember to include both elements in our painting to keep the picture in perspective. And we owe it to one another to keep our mental image a "work in progress," because that's what all of us are.

Clue 2: Focus on What You Do When You're Not Disagreeing

If you've ever tried to carry a glass brim-full of water, you know how hard it is to carry without its spilling over. The trick is to never look at the glass but to focus instead on your destination, and the glass will remain level.

In steering a car around a curve, a beginning driver will stare at the road directly in front of the car and tug at the wheel in awkward jerks. The better method is to fix your eyes on the road far ahead, and the car will ease smoothly around the bend.

In marriage we often make a similar error in focus. If the quantity or style of disagreement between us is a cause for concern, then we bring our full attention to bear on our *conflicts*. What are we doing wrong here? How do we fix this? Why do we keep having this problem, and what do we need to change? We focus intensely on the problem, but the problem doesn't seem to go away. The glass spills over, and the car lurches forward, and we're still not sure what's wrong.

As strange as it sounds, most arguments occur because of what we do when we're *not* arguing. If you're trying to extend grace to each other every day, if you're working to create a constant atmosphere of love and goodwill, then—surprise! The amount of conflict in your marriage will strangely diminish without focusing on conflict at all. But if there's coldness and distance between you, if your daily communication is sparse and abrupt, then your next conversation is an argument waiting to happen.

Sometimes life gets so busy that marriage begins to feel

more like a business partnership—two co-owners both punching a time clock, both putting in as much overtime as possible just to make sure the business keeps running. The only time we see each other is when there's a business crisis, and then it's only long enough to pick up the pieces and hurry back to our respective duties.

We need time together to build our marriages—time to do the things that originally caused us to fall in love. We need time to talk about our conflicts, yes—but we also need time to talk about anything *other* than conflict. Scott Stanley writes:

> Just as it's important to set aside times to deal with issues in your relationship, it's critical that you set aside times for enjoying the God-given blessings of marriage. You can't be focusing on issues all the time and have a really great marriage. You need some nurturing and safe times for relaxing—having fun, talking as friends, making love—when conflict and problems are always off limits.[4]

It was Socrates who told us, "The unexamined life isn't worth living." What he neglected to add was, "The *over-*examined life is no better." If you're planning to solve your ongoing conflicts by concentrating on them until they go away, good luck. Your very focus may intensify the problem, just as rays of sunlight burn deeper when condensed by a magnifier. The best way to resolve a conflict is to *pre*-solve it, by investing in the quality of the relationship itself.

Clue 3: Never Give Up Hope

The Bible has a lot to say about hope, because hope is such a powerful, preserving force in our lives. Hope is a child of love itself. "Love never gives up," Paul wrote, "never loses faith, is always hopeful, and endures through every circumstance" (1 Corinthians 13:7 NLT). But the truth is, sometimes we *do* lose hope, and when we do, the road ahead is much more difficult .

How many times have you and your mate committed to begin a new program, set a new schedule, or make a fresh start, only to forget all about it just a few weeks later? How many times have you agreed to change the way you talk, listen, or disagree, just to return to your old habits in record time? That kind of sudden starting and stopping is hard on a vehicle, and it's hard on hearts as well. "Hope deferred makes the heart sick," Proverbs 13:12 reminds us, and after endless cycles of hope and disappointment you may be suffering from a case of "heartsickness." The symptoms include doubt, discouragement, and skepticism. At the very mention of a new plan, project, or program, you begin to experience a sinking feeling in the pit of your stomach. "What's the point?" you ask yourself. "Why bother? Why should *this* time be any different?"

This may not be the first book you've read on conflict resolution, and it's certainly not the first time you've attempted to make an improvement in your marriage. How do you keep a sense of hopefulness after all those past disappointments? What's supposed to keep you *going*?

Two things can help us to stay hopeful about our marriages. First of all, we need to ask ourselves whom we're disappointed *in*. We should be disappointed in *us*. *We* failed to stick to our new program; *we* need to do better next time. Remember the log in your own eye: The truth is, you both share *some* responsibility for not making the changes you wanted to make. But in our anger and frustration, we often place the disappointment squarely on our mates. We say, "*You* failed to keep your commitment; *you* didn't do what you said you would do." But your mate may believe that the lion's share of the blame belongs to *you*. When you each place the entire fault on the other, you both begin a downward spiral of blame shifting and faultfinding, and that only adds to the atmosphere of hopelessness.

The second thing we can do to remain hopeful is to remember whom our hope is *in*. "Find rest, O my soul, in God alone," the psalmist writes, "my hope comes from him" (Psalm 62:5 NIV). Husbands will fail and wives will disappoint, but God's purposes still remain. The focus of our hope should be that God is intent on finishing the work that He began in your husband's life, not that your husband will finally get his act together. "For it is God who is at work in you, both to will and to work for His good pleasure" (Philippians 2:13).

When you feel yourself beginning to lose hope, remember that you're probably not alone. Your mate may be suffering from a form of heartsickness very similar to yours—and from exactly the same source. The most touching series of responses to our survey was in reply to the question, "The one thing I wish my mate understood about me is . . ." Listen to the responses of some fellow patients from the Heartsick Ward . . .

- *I am on his side.*
- *I'm harder on myself than she could ever be.*
- *All I want is for him to love me.*
- *I am weird, and sometimes I can't be explained. Even I don't have an explanation.*
- *I wish she could understand how hard I am trying to keep things going.*
- *I wish he knew how much I love him and how much I want oneness in our marriage.*
- *I wish she knew that I love her and desire her even when I don't express it properly.*

Many of the respondents to our survey longed for their mates to know how much they loved them, how hard they were trying, and how frustrated and confused they felt sometimes. Over and over again the message was, "I do care, and you are not the only one hoping for things to improve."

Fight the temptation to surrender hope in your marriage. Remember that your mate may need encouragement too. By keeping hope we create *possibilities*. We need to constantly encourage each other with the thought that *this could work*. Susan Page reminds us,

> You may become discouraged if you don't see major transformations right away. Just remember, it is perfectly normal to become discouraged when you try something and it doesn't work the first time. Let yourself feel disappointed; *just don't let your disappointment stop you from going on.*5

This time *can* be different—but only if you think it can. You can give up on a technique, or a program, or a schedule, but never give up on each other—and never give up hope.

What is the answer to our "riddle within a riddle"? What do we mean by the principle, "Don't live with conflict, live with your mate"? "Don't live with conflict" means to refuse to allow your disagreements to color your view of the entire relationship. "Live with your mate" means to spend your time and energy on building a good marriage, not just on the problems between you. And most of all, "Don't live with conflict, live with your mate" means to never give up hope—in your marriage, in your mate, and in the One who sustains you both.

* * *

We were once in a checkout line at a large department store, and an older couple was standing in front of us. The woman said something that her male companion didn't comprehend, and so he said quietly, "I don't understand."

With this, the woman turned to the man and glared. She took a deep breath and began to speak in a voice that made quite certain that he and everyone else in the store would hear this time.

She said, "Of *course* you don't understand! You never *have* understood, and you never *will!*"

Everyone in the store instinctively dropped his eyes in an effort to help the man preserve whatever dignity he could. As we looked down, we noticed that the man and woman were both wearing gold wedding bands. This was not a feud between rival business partners or a spat between frustrated siblings; this was a husband and wife. They were not a part of the national divorce statistic; they were still living "happily ever after." They were exactly the sort of couple we might honor at a marriage conference when we ask, "Who here has been married the longest?"

And suddenly a thought occurred to us: *Not all fiftieth anniversaries are golden.*

The Longing for Intimacy

Marriage is not a Frequent Flier program. No one will give you a free trip to the Bahamas just for logging marital miles. What we all long for most, deep in our hearts, is not merely longevity, but *love.*

The greatest mistake that a couple can make is to confuse *proximity* with *intimacy. They are not the same.* We yearn for intimacy, and so we marry. Once we're married, we assume that we have automatically achieved our goal. After all, we *live* together, we *sleep* together—how could two people be this close and not be intimate? Sadly, millions of couples can answer that question from firsthand experience.

Marriage makes intimacy possible, but not inevitable. Entering a marriage will not satisfy your hunger for companionship any more than entering a restaurant will satisfy your hunger for food. Too many couples make the mistake of viewing their wedding day as the end of a race—the race to find a mate—instead of hearing the words "I now pronounce you husband and wife" as the starting gun in a lifelong race to become intimate. Every couple begins this race, but not every

287

couple finishes it. After fifty years of marriage, every couple crosses a major milestone in that race; for many, it is not the golden event they had imagined.

Our purpose in writing *The Seven Conflicts* is to encourage couples everywhere to resume the race for their original goal—true intimacy. That goal will require a new approach to conflict, both in attitude and action. We'd like to recommend the following list as a summary of the attitudes and actions necessary to finish that race and finish it well:

I will not be ashamed by the presence of conflict in my marriage.

I will work to see the good side of my mate's different dreams and values.

I will choose to see my mate's differences as tools God uses to shape me into the person He intends me to be.

I will not resent my mate for the shaping role he plays in my life.

I will seek to be an ambassador of goodwill in thought and deed.

I will not hide from conflict.

I will try to identify my part in the problem. I will look for the log in my own eye before I look for the speck in hers.

I will approach our disagreements and differences with an attitude of humility.

I will abandon dead-end approaches to conflict and seek more productive methods.

I will seek to become a master packager. I will speak the truth in love.

I will do my best to constantly move toward the fence, and I will encourage my mate to do the same.

I will not let our problems dominate my focus. I will concentrate on loving my mate and building a great marriage.

The suggestions in this book are only the beginning of a lifelong journey—a journey *away* from the excesses of your own personality and *toward* the strange and mysterious world of your partner in marriage. But the journey of a thousand miles begins with a single step, so we've offered some simple first steps that you can use to begin to move toward the fence. There is nothing magical about these suggestions. Perhaps the most important thing is that you take a step at all.

Whether or not the ideas in this book work for you will be determined by your attitude, your style, your persistence, and most of all by God's grace. As the Lord reminded Joshua, "Do not be terrified; do not be discouraged, for the LORD your God will be with you wherever you go" (1:9 NIV).

Notes

Chapter 1

1. John Gottman and Nan Silver, *The Seven Principles for Making Marriage Work* (New York: Three Rivers Press, 1999), 129.
2. Ibid., 130.

Chapter 2

1. Scott Stanley et al., *A Lasting Promise: A Christian Guide to Fighting for Your Marriage* (San Francisco: Jossey-Bass, 1998), 119, 135, 129.
2. Ibid., 119.
3. Clifford Notarius and Howard Markman, *We Can Work It Out: How to Solve Conflicts, Save Your Marriage, and Strengthen Your Love for Each Other* (New York: Putnam, 1993), 153.

Chapter 4

1. Terry Hargrave and Nedra Fetterman, "The Ineffable Us-ness of Marriage," *Psychotherapy Networker*, July/August 2001 (Vol. 25, No. 4), 55–61.
2. Michael Leach and Therese Borchard, eds., *I Like Being Married: Treasured Traditions, Rituals, and Stories* (New York: Doubleday, 2002).

Chapter 6

1. Susan Page, *How One of You Can Bring the Two of You Together: Breakthrough Strategies to Resolve Your Conflicts and Reignite Your Love* (New York: Broadway Books, 1997), 155.

Chapter 8

1. For more on introversion and extroversion, see David Keirsey and Marilyn Bates, *Please Understand Me: Character and Temperament Types* (Del Mar, Calif.: Prometheus Nemesis, 1984), 14–16.

2. Julia Wood, *Interpersonal Communication: Everyday Encounters,* 2d Ed. (Belmont, Calif.: Wadsworth, 1999), 253.

Chapter 10

1. Dan Allender and Tremper Longman, *Intimate Allies: Rediscovering God's Design for Marriage and Becoming Soul Mates for Life* (Wheaton, Ill.: Tyndale, 1995), 73.

2. Ibid.

3. Ibid., 82.

4. Thomas Moore, *Soul Mates* (New York: HarperCollins, 1994), 237.

5. Ibid., 234.

6. Allender and Longman, *Intimate Allies,* 345.

7. Ibid., 44.

Chapter 11

1. John Gottman and Nan Silver, *The Seven Principles for Making Marriage Work* (New York: Three Rivers Press, 1999), 158–59.

2. Susan Page, *How One of You Can Bring the Two of You Together: Breakthrough Strategies to Resolve Your Conflicts and Reignite Your Love* (New York: Broadway Books, 1997), 5–6.

3. Deborah Tannen, *You Just Don't Understand: Women and Men in Conversation* (New York: Ballantine Books, 1990), 25.

4. Ibid.

5. Rebecca Cutter, *When Opposites Attract: Right Brain / Left Brain Relationships and How to Make Them Work* (New York: Dutton, 1994), 92.

6. Ibid., 53.

7. Larry Crabb, "The Real Problem," *Bring Home the Joy* (Grand Rapids: Zondervan, 1998), 85.

8. Page, *How One of You Can Bring the Two of You Together,* 33.

9. Cutter, *When Opposites Attract,* 92–93.

Chapter 12

1. Michele Weiner-Davis, *Divorce Busting: A Step-By-Step Approach to Making Your Marriage Loving Again* (New York: Simon & Schuster, 1992), 100–101.
2. Ibid., 101.
3. John Gottman, *The Seven Principles for Making Marriage Work* (New York: Three Rivers Press, 1999), 27.
4. Sybil Evans and Sherry Cohen, *Hot Buttons: How to Resolve Conflict and Cool Everyone Down* (New York: Cliff Street Books, 2000).

Chapter 13

1. David Keirsey and Marilyn Bates, *Please Understand Me: Character and Temperament Types* (Del Mar, Calif.: Prometheus Nemesis, 1984), 2.
2. Ibid.

Chapter 14

1. Eric Hoffer, *Reflections on the Human Condition* (New York: Harper Collins, 1973), aphorism 144.
2. James Walker, *Husbands Who Won't Lead and Wives Who Won't Follow* (Minneapolis: Bethany House, 1989), 88.

Chapter 16

1. David Keirsey and Marilyn Bates, *Please Understand Me: Character and Temperament Types* (Del Mar, Calif.: Prometheus Nemesis, 1984), 16.

Chapter 17

1. Eric Hoffer, *The Passionate State of Mind* (Cutchogue, N.Y.: Buccaneer, 1955), aphorism 262.
2. David Keirsey and Marilyn Bates, *Please Understand Me: Character and Temperament Types* (Del Mar, Calif.: Prometheus Nemesis, 1984), 2.
3. Michele Weiner-Davis, *Divorce Busting: A Step-By-Step Approach to Making Your Marriage Loving Again* (New York: Simon & Schuster, 1992), 126.
4. Scott Stanley et al., *A Lasting Promise: A Christian Guide to Fighting for Your Marriage* (San Francisco: Jossey Bass, 1998), 109.

5. Susan Page, *How One of You Can Bring the Two of You Together: Breakthrough Strategies to Resolve Your Conflicts and Reignite Your Love* (New York: Broadway Books, 1997), 20.

BIBLIOGRAPHY

Allender, Dan and Tremper Longman. *Intimate Allies: Redis-covering God's Design for Marriage and Becoming Soul Mates for Life.* Wheaton, Ill.: Tyndale, 1995.

Baxter, Leslie and Barbara Montgomery. *Relating: Dialogues and Dialectics.* New York: Guilford, 1996.

Chapman, Gary. *The Five Love Languages: How to Express Heartfelt Commitment to Your Mate.* Chicago: Northfield, 1995.

Christensen, Andrew and Neil Jacobson. *Reconcilable Differ-ences.* New York: Guilford, 2000.

Cutter, Rebecca. *When Opposites Attract: Right Brain / Left Brain Relationships and How to Make Them Work.* New York: Dutton, 1994.

Dodds, Elisabeth. *Marriage to a Difficult Man: The Uncom-mon Union of Jonathan and Sarah Edwards.* Louisville: Westminster John Knox Press, 1903.

Evans, Sybil and Sherry Cohen. *Hot Buttons: How to Resolve Conflict and Cool Everyone Down.* New York: Cliff Street Books, 2000.

Gottman, John and Nan Silver. *The Seven Principles for Mak-ing Marriage Work.* New York: Three Rivers Press, 1999.

Gottman, John. *Why Marriages Succeed or Fail . . . and How You Can Make Yours Last.* New York: Fireside, 1994.

Hoffer, Eric. *The Passionate State of Mind.* Cutchogue, N.Y.: Buccaneer Books, 1955.

Hoffer, Eric. *Reflections on the Human Condition.* New York: HarperCollins, 1973.

Keirsey, David and Marilyn Bates. *Please Understand Me: Character and Temperament Types.* Del Mar, Calif.: Prometheus Nemesis, 1984.

Lickson, Charles. *Ironing it Out: Seven Simple Steps to Resolving Conflict.* Menlo Park, Calif.: Crisp Publications, 1996.

Moore, Thomas. *Soul Mates.* New York: HarperCollins, 1994.

Notarius, Clifford and Howard Markman. *We Can Work It Out: How to Solve Conflicts, Save Your Marriage, and Strengthen Your Love for Each Other.* New York: Penguin Putnam Inc., 1993.

Page, Susan. *How One of You Can Bring the Two of You Together: Breakthrough Strategies to Resolve Your Conflicts and Reignite Your Love.* New York: Broadway Books, 1997.

Springer, Sally and Georg Deutsch. *Left Brain / Right Brain,* 4th ed. New York: W.H. Freeman and Company, 1993.

Stanley, Scott, Daniel Trathen, Savanna McCain, and Milt Bryan. *A Lasting Promise: A Christian Guide to Fighting for Your Marriage.* San Francisco: Jossey Bass, 1998.

Tannen, Deborah. *You Just Don't Understand: Women and Men in Conversation.* New York: Ballantine, 1990.

Ury, William. *Getting to Peace: Transforming Conflict at Home, at Work, and in the World.* New York: Viking, 1999.

Walker, James. *Husbands Who Won't Lead and Wives Who Won't Follow.* Minneapolis: Bethany House, 1989.

Weeks, Dudley. *The Eight Essential Steps to Conflict Resolution: Preserving Relationships at Work, at Home, and in the Community.* New York: Putnam, 1994.

Weiner-Davis, Michele. *Divorce Busting: A Step-By-Step Approach to Making Your Marriage Loving Again.* New York: Simon & Schuster, 1992.

Women of Faith, ed. *Bring Home the Joy.* Grand Rapids: Zondervan, 1998.

Wood, Julia. *Interpersonal Communication: Everyday Encounters,* 2d Ed. Belmont, Calif.: Wadsworth, 1999.

SINCE 1894, Moody Publishers has been dedicated to equip and motivate people to advance the cause of Christ by publishing evangelical Christian literature and other media for all ages, around the world. Because we are a ministry of the Moody Bible Institute of Chicago, a portion of the proceeds from the sale of this book go to train the next generation of Christian leaders.

If we may serve you in any way in your spiritual journey toward understanding Christ and the Christian life, please contact us at www.moodypublishers.com.

"All Scripture is God-breathed and is useful for teaching, rebuking, correcting and training in righteousness, so that the man of God may be thoroughly equipped for every good work."

—2 TIMOTHY 3:16, 17

MOODY
PUBLISHERS

THE NAME YOU CAN TRUST®